NO PEACE UNTIL HE'S DEAD

NO PEACE UNTIL
HE'S DEAD

Amanda Brown was born in Belfast and grew up in Ballymoney. She was thrust into the public eye when she took the stand to give evidence against her stepfather Davy Tweed, former Ireland and Ulster rugby player, and her brave testimony went a long way to securing his conviction on a litany of serious sex abuse charges. She has since engaged with the Department of Justice and the Victims of Crime Commission, and Victim Support NI, as part of her work advocating for other survivors of sexual abuse. She is now a qualified reflexologist and aromatherapist, and her business is registered as a safe space for victims of domestic violence.

NO PEACE UNTIL HE'S DEAD

My Story of Child Abuse at the Hands of
Davy Tweed and My Journey to Recovery

AMANDA BROWN

MERRION
PRESS

First published in 2024 by
Merrion Press
10 George's Street
Newbridge
Co. Kildare
Ireland
www.merrionpress.ie

978 1 78537 498 2 (Paper)
978 1 78537 499 9 (Ebook)

A CIP catalogue record for this book is available from the British Library.

Typeset in Sabon LT Pro 11.5/18

Cover design by Fiachra McCarthy.

Merrion Press is a member of Publishing Ireland.

For Gemma

Contents

Prologue

The many missed calls and twenty texts from my brother were unusual, so I called him straight back.

'Who's dead?' I said when I heard him answer. I was joking, but I knew something was up.

He took a breath.

'Davy,' he said.

I inhaled sharply. 'Davy who?' I asked. I knew who, but the room had started spinning. I needed confirmation.

'Davy Tweed,' my brother said, and the room stopped spinning with a jolt.

Davy Tweed was sixty-one when he was killed while riding his motorbike along a quiet road in Dunseverick. Apparently over-taking, he lost control, despite good conditions and dry roads. They said he snapped his neck.

I wondered what it felt like to hit the tarmac. I thought about that for a long time, I tried to imagine his last moments, I tried to imagine his death. What way he might have fallen ... and if he had suffered. My brother said he was killed instantly, but I was bothered by that. Apparently, the paramedics did try to revive him and I clung to that, hoping he was conscious at least long enough for his life to flash before his eyes. Did he think about me? Did he regret what he did? Did he hear the screeches and howls of the demons in hell as his neck took his weight and ended him there and then? Did he lie there dying and wish he could change it?

Did it even matter?

My brother gave me all the details he had.

'It happened last night,' he said. 'I rang you, but the phone was off.'

'My battery died.' I was sorry, I knew that he would have wanted to make sure he gave me the news before I saw it on the front of the paper or had a neighbour break it to me.

'How do you feel?' he asked.

'I don't know,' I said.

I think what I felt was relief, perhaps, and worry for my mum, worry for my family, knowing that we would be dragged into this either way.

'Where did it happen?' I asked.

'Whitepark Bay Road,' he said.

'Jesus,' I said, 'I was only just up there.'

I was surprised. Not long before Davy's fatal accident I had been driving on that road and I had stopped to admire a field full of sunflowers. It was a bright warm day and I spent a while walking among the giant flowers, watching the way they swayed, their thick stems holding the large yellow heads full of seeds. The sound of bees filled the air, and the sun fed them, and me.

I felt so tiny there, among the towering flowers. Someone had picked seeds from one whose head was bent down as if in a greeting, the stolen seeds made a smiling face. It was amusing and sweet.

There was a sign there, left on the ground near the entrance. It read, 'That which stands tall casts a long shadow', and although I knew it was a metaphor for living well, for honesty and principles, it made me think of the opposite.

Davy Tweed was tall. And his shadow was terrifying.

I realised my wish had come true. This death was one that I had called on the universe for many times. I had dreamed about being at his deathbed, with him begging me for forgiveness. Sometimes in those dreams, I gave my forgiveness, releasing him from his burdens before he passed away. Sometimes, I finished him off myself. I wondered if he ever felt remorse and thought about seeking me out to apologise. But I knew that was not who he was, not at all. In some ways how he died was how he lived, taking what he wanted.

I called my sisters one by one. They were waiting for confirmation and holding their breath. Their voices were low and stressed. I told them what I knew: that they would feel many things and all of those feelings were okay to feel. This was a complicated thing.

Then I called my mum. She didn't say much, but I talked to her and said all the right things.

At ten o'clock the news broke. I read the headlines – 'Former Rugby International David Tweed Killed in Motorbike Crash' – then sat down heavily on the chair and exhaled.

I went onto Facebook and posted: Convicted paedophile dies following a motorbike accident.

1

Childhood Lost

David Tweed was a railway engineer for most of his life, apprenticed to his father. He was married twice, the second time to my mother, Margaret – his first wife was never mentioned. He grew up on a farm, loved Status Quo, fry-ups and his motorbike. He was a politician, a member of the Grand Orange Order, the Apprentice Boys of Derry and the Black Preceptory. He was an international rugby player for Ireland.

Davy Tweed was my stepfather.

Davy Tweed was a wife-beater.

Davy Tweed was a child molester.

Davy Tweed was a monster.

My parents had been together since they were fourteen. By the time they were old enough to vote, they were already parents and, encouraged to do the right thing by their elders, they got married. They moved into a standard, small, terraced house in White City on Whitewell Road, in North Belfast. My dad worked in an electronics repair shop and my mum worked in Crazy Prices. They were too young I suppose, playing house, children having children, and my father eventually broke my mother's heart. She moved out with me and my brother to her sister's flat, now a single parent having to cope on her own. That was how things were for us.

I have memories of the home we lived in with my dad. I remember high hedges around the house and a wooden gate. The walls were patterned inside, orange and brown. I remember being sick once, down with a bug. I was wrapped up in a blanket and carried to the couch, and the TV was put on for me. My mother brought me Lucozade in a foil-covered bottle and felt the temperature of my forehead with the palm of her hand.

My dad was an avid photographer, always taking pictures, and he used the smallest room upstairs as a darkroom. He would disappear in there for hours and come out with photographs of us on shiny paper that he would frame and hang. I have some of those still, and I cherish them.

We played in the back garden in the summer, in a paddling pool blown up by my dad or Uncle Danny, who was not much older than us – there are less than eight years between him and me, but he was a 'big boy' back then. We would be stripped down to our pants and given homemade ice pops on sticks that would melt and run down your hand.

We ran around outside, thudding balls off the wall, playing chase. The milkman would come around in the mornings and sometimes my mum would let us have some orange juice off him. I have never since managed to find orange juice like it – it was delicious.

My mum and dad would sometimes bring us up to Belfast Castle, where we would run up the hill holding mum's hand and climb up the green stairs at Hazelbank Park. Other times they'd bring us to Browns Bay, and we would make footprints in the sand and watch as the sea came in and rubbed them out.

In that house we had a Scalextric set – got for Christmas – and Danny would come over to play with it. We were cute and mischievous children when my parents were together, always up to something. I remember my brother dipped the Scalextric car in a tub of chocolate mousse we had been given to eat, then put it back on the track and raced it, making me laugh as thick blobs of mousse flew everywhere.

'Ack now, that's a waste of a good dessert,' Mum said when she came in to see what we were laughing at. She took the car away and rinsed it off in the sink. 'If you do that again, I'll take the set off ye,' she called from the kitchen. We sometimes got told off like that – warned to be good – but we never worried deeply, not back then. We weren't afraid of Mum and Dad.

Another day, when I was around three years old, I told my dad I was off up to call for the wee girl next door.

'You can't,' he said to me. 'There's thunder and lightning outside, you'll get a fright.'

I didn't know what thunder and lightning were. I was just up out of bed and wanting to play.

'I'm not afraid of that,' I said. I stuck my chin up to show that I was well able.

'Well if you want to go, go,' Dad said, 'but don't say I didn't warn you.'

I barely made it to the corner of the street before I heard a crash and bang in the sky above me and the whole place lit up with a flash. I screamed and ran like hell, back into the house, back into my dad's arms as he laughed and picked me up and said, 'I told you you'd get a fright, but you didn't listen to your daddy now, did you?'

I loved the feeling of being in my dad's arms.

I remember dinner, hot in bowls on the table, with the four of us together. The smell of cooking onions brings me back to that table with us all together, when everything was alright and all was well. My favourite was mince in gravy, with dots of carrots my mum had chopped into it, poured steaming over hot buttered spuds. My mouth wasn't big enough for the huge spoonfuls I forced into it.

'Small bites now, love,' Mum would say.

Once it snowed and Mum dressed us up in boots and snowsuits that made it impossible to turn your head or put your arms by your side. We stood like stars, entranced by the white fluff falling from the sky as it landed thick around us, then made snowballs and snowmen, running back and forth crunching the ice beneath our boots.

I was loved and safe and happy. It was a childhood that didn't last.

I started nursery school not long before my parents split. My mum would bring me down, holding my hand, and pick me up too. One of the only clear memories I have was a dress-up day, and I wanted to be a mermaid for it. I've no idea if the costume succeeded or what it was made of – I just remember being dressed up at school and that there was a barbecue, which was something I'd never seen. It made a huge impression on me, eating burgers outside in the sunshine with my parents and my brother; it felt wonderful. Years later I would meet a woman on a course and – after chatting for a while – she realised we had gone to nursery school together. She brought in a photo of the class and there I was. It would have been taken not long before everything changed.

The child in that photo was happy and innocent, with contented parents. But my dad cheated on my mother a few months later and that changed everything.

I don't think people realise the ripple effects of such things, not at the time anyway; how selfish decisions can lead to entire lives being changed for ever.

When my parents split up, my mum moved with us into my Aunt Olivia's house, which was just at the end of the street where our own house had been. My dad moved to England not long afterwards. Olivia's place was a flat on the first floor of a block, the kind that has shops running along in a row on the ground floor.

I was barely four.

I remember there was a sweet shop directly underneath my aunt's flat, and so this new life, at first, seemed pretty ideal to me. I was allowed down on my own when I got my pocket money to buy sweeties. I loved Sherbert Dip, those cardboard tubes full of fizzy powder with a stick of liquorice to suck and dip in.

There was also a chip shop, the old-fashioned kind that had a glass jar of pickled eggs on the counter, which I would be given as a treat for helping my aunt carry her bottles down from her flat to get the ten cents a bottle offered at the time for recycling.

Granny and Grandpa's house was nearby too, off Whitewell Road in Pineview Gardens, a little estate built on a hill backing on to Belfast Zoo. You could hear lions roaring from their back door. It was a red-brick house with a side passage that we took to get to the back door. We didn't need to knock.

Granny was a seamstress, constantly sewing clothes for her family, and most days when you entered her house you would hear the pummel and whirr of the machine on the landing upstairs and know where to find her. Some days there would be no whirr and you'd find her perched on the sofa smoking a cigarette, and she would promise to make you a 'jam piece' as soon as she was done. And she would, buttering a slice of bread and adding jam and putting it straight into your hand without the formality of a plate. A moment later you'd be given a glass of milk to go with it.

My grandparents' house was bigger than ours, with three bedrooms upstairs and two reception rooms downstairs. Her younger children were still living there when I was small. Family would sit in the back room, by the kitchen, on soft mustard-coloured couches, while 'guests' would get the privilege of the 'good room' where the fancy settee was – dark swirls of florals on velvet – along with ornaments and family photos. She had those white porcelain dogs, the ones everyone had, on each end of her mantelpiece and a painting of a lady on the wall.

When I was very small, when my mum and dad were married, formal visits would be on Sunday, with others dotted throughout the week as my mum popped in for a quick hello, maybe on her way to her sister's. There was always a pot of something, stew or soup maybe, on the cooker, and big bowls of unpeeled cooked spuds to help yourself to. The sounds of that house on Sundays – which was the day everyone called in – were voices, laughter and the clink of spoons in bowls, kids at the kitchen table, grown-ups on the couch, everyone getting on and living their lives.

On weekends, Granny drank Bacardi, often poured into a tin of orange pop. I remember once trying to convince her that I loved orange pop, even though she kept telling me I wouldn't like it, and

I went on and on until she let me take a sip. One was enough! On Saturdays she often drank too much and would end up spending Sunday in bed recovering.

That was a normal thing in my childhood, being told Granny was staying in bed, and you'd go up there to see her. She would often be in a terrible state, more extreme than a regular hangover. It never mattered much. The house was still as warm and safe as ever, even when she wasn't well.

Granny would boil up huge sides of beef ribs. I loved the way the meat fell off into my mouth and I'd gnaw the bone to get the last bits. On Sundays she would make huge bowls of stew, the easiest option for the constant stream of relatives coming in and out, and at the times when the house was filled with all of us, she would sit the littlest ones at the table and give us hot bowls of soup or stew with a potato in the middle of it. The soup was boiled for hours with a ham hock in it, so there would be little bits of salty ham floating in there. You'd spend your time searching for them with your spoon instead of drinking it up. There was something satisfying about finding the small pink flecks of ham.

Aunt Olivia had a daughter, Jessica, who was two years younger than me.[1] Living with her cemented a bond between us that we have never lost. We were always together as we grew up, like sisters. When we were small our mums dressed us alike and matched us on things like Christmas outfits and even presents. If I got a

---

1 I have changed many of the names in this book to preserve the privacy of those involved in these events.

Barbie, so would Jessica, which meant we would play together all the time. She was my first best friend, like a sister would be.

That time, living with Olivia, was my last moment of childhood. It was the last time I had the safety and care of the adults around me. It was the time before Davy Tweed. When he came through our door, everything changed – for me, for my mum, for everyone.

We never had much as kids, even when my dad was still around, but what we did have was a childhood. We had freedom and innocence and fun.

Davy Tweed took all of that away.

I wish he had never been born. If he had never existed, I would not have this heavy burden to carry at all.

2

A New 'Family'

When I was really little I would wake in the night in a dark room and I would feel as though I was being suffocated under a heavy weight. I couldn't move, caught under something, crushed into the mattress. I couldn't hear, I couldn't see, I couldn't speak. I always told my mum the next day and she would shush me and pat me and tell me they were nightmares and not to worry. But I did worry. I would feel really scared going to bed at night in case it would happen again.

There was something in my room in the nighttime that was bad, and I was afraid of it.

Perhaps it was a night terror, perhaps it was a waking reality, but whatever it was, my life was completely different from what it had been. My father was gone, the home I knew was closed to me, and my mother was being battered by her partner, Davy Tweed.

My mother met Davy at a wedding, not long after she split from my dad. Newly separated and living in her sister's spare room with her two kids, it wasn't surprising that he swept her off her feet. My mother was brokenhearted, lonely and a single mother. So when Davy galloped in on his white horse, taking us two kids on as his own, a knight in shining armour who worked hard, played a sport and promised to provide her and her children with a good life, it was impossible to resist.

Davy was born in a small rural village between Ballymena and Ballymoney called Dunloy. His father was a railway engineer and they also kept a small farm, which instilled in Davy the dedication and early starts that he needed to become a rugby player. Davy worked on that farm his whole childhood and then joined his father on the railways as an apprentice engineer, working shifts both day and night. And, of course, he played rugby – for his local team and then for Ireland.

Davy had been married before, but we knew nothing about it. He never talked about his ex-wife. Never mentioned her by name.

It was all too perfect, all too much like a fairy tale. Irresistible. My mum wanted a traditional life. And so did Davy. He moved us in with him so quickly.

Davy was fun, at first, waking us up on Saturday mornings playing air guitar to Status Quo, dancing into our bedrooms laughing at us as we woke up.

'Look at youse!' he would say. 'Sleepy heads on youse!'

He was the fun dad, the silly dad. We loved him, at first, running to him when he came in from work.

'Call me Daddy, alright?' he said. So we did.

We didn't hesitate to give Davy back the love he bombed us with. We thought it was real.

To everyone else it looked like the perfect story.

But the truth of our family quickly became very different.

Behind the closed doors of our bungalow in Ballymoney, my

mother was being battered, dragged across the floor by the hair, kicked into corners of the room, snarled at and shaken. No matter what she did, nothing was good enough.

And behind the closed doors of our bungalow Davy Tweed was also abusing his children.

Mum kept a good house, clean and tidy. She made good food, dinners that Davy liked, and had it hot on the table when he came in. Every evening, after we had gone to bed, she stood in the kitchen making his lunch for the following day. But she couldn't know what mark or wrinkle he would find after scanning the room for a while; she couldn't foresee that the spoon in the sink would upset him when it never had before, or that the fingerprint on the window – mine – would be too much for him to bear.

'I am out there morning, noon and night, working my ass off to keep this house,' he would say, 'and your only job is to cook and clean … and you can't even do that.'

Mum would apologise, try to make amends, feeling a pressure she wasn't used to. Not knowing how to breathe this air. Not realising she was being groomed for abuse. She tried to submit, tried to be better. She was being worn down.

'I pulled you from the gutter,' he would hiss against her face as he dragged her down the hall away from us to continue the conversation. 'You were nothing, nobody else would want a single mother …'

When men get you like that, fragile and broken-hearted, they can make you feel like nothing, and feel it so deeply that you believe what they say, that you're worthless, a piece of shit that nobody would want. And women are told from the day they are born that their value lies in their ability to keep a man, so how can I not understand my mother? How could she have thought straight at all with years of being spoken to like that, years of being brainwashed into believing she was what he said?

Words hurled at her, then fists.

She told me later that the first time he hit her was because she made Davy jealous. She made him jealous. Is that the deal we get? Women being responsible for men's reactions?

We were living then in a small square in Ballymoney with Davy's sister Rose, isolated from our own people in Belfast, surrounded by mostly elderly couples. We never saw our own aunts and uncles; we just saw Davy's family.

My mum told me that our bike tyres had low pressure, so herself and Rose were fixing them out the front. The weather was good, we were playing in the square and my mum, who was still in her twenties, took one of the bikes and Rose took the other and they set off cycling them around the square, laughing and messing, just as Davy came up the road.

Perhaps it was the sight of my mother in a moment where she looked happy and free-spirited, or perhaps it was the presence of a man who was walking his dog and looking on with a smile, but Davy was immediately filled with rage. He ordered my mum back into the house, and once he got her in there he dragged her upstairs by the scruff of her neck, she told me, and punched her.

'Don't take me for a fool,' he said to her, 'your man out there with the dog ...'

She swore to him that she wasn't doing anything at all but messing with Rose, but he punched her again.

'I know about you and your fellas,' he apparently said to her as he dragged her along the hall, 'a friend of mine told me I'm living with a slut!'

Not long after that he moved us into a home of our own, where my mum was more isolated, more vulnerable. The new house had two storeys and was in the Carnany estate in Ballymoney. It had stairs on the left when you went in and a kitchen at the back. There was a small living room and a kitchen dinette, a small garden at the back, closed in, and at the front there was a communal space, sectioned off in parts with low fences. An alley ran along behind the back gardens, giving access. Up the top was a play park and beyond that were fields with cows. We were given permission to go to the play park alone – the independence was exciting and we loved the new house, not only for that but because we each, my brother and I, had a room of our own.

My room was painted immediately, a dusty pink, and Strawberry Shortcake wallpaper was put on one wall. My brother's room was painted blue. It was just the two of us and we were delighted. But it wasn't just the two of us for long, as my mum quickly fell pregnant. Davy was delighted and hoped for a boy. Mum did too, thinking maybe he wouldn't be so angry, maybe the baby would calm things down. Surely now he would know she wasn't having affairs, she wasn't unfaithful.

One evening Davy went to the clubhouse of his rugby team to drink. His wife ran a bath to ease her pregnancy aches and pains. My brother and I were in bed. When Davy arrived back and couldn't find his front door key, he went around to the back door, only to find it locked. He went back to the front door, instantly enraged, and began banging and kicking the door until it nearly gave way. My mum ran down and opened the door and was met by this charging bull, who dragged her up the stairs by the hair and back into the bathroom, fists flying, anger spitting filth from his lips. She was twenty-four, pregnant and trapped. And he beat her. But in the way of so-called 'domestics', when the police were called by the neighbours, as became a pattern with Davy and his wife, they would arrive, then simply shrug and leave, each and every time.

A few weeks later, on a normal day, all hell suddenly broke loose in the house as my mother realised that the stomach pain that had made her bear down on the toilet was actually labour. She managed to catch the baby before she hit the bowl.

We were playing out on the street when Davy called us in. 'You two get into Aaron's room there,' he said, 'and shut that door and don't so much as peek out until someone comes for you.'

By this time we were scared of Davy. So we stayed in there, listening to the sounds of Davy going up and down the stairs.

'Where are the children?' we heard Davy's sister Sharon ask from the landing – she was going in and out of the bathroom too.

'They're in there,' we heard Davy say.

Eventually, we heard the sounds of an ambulance outside, at which point we ran to the window. We watched our mother, wrapped in a foil blanket, as she was wheeled down the path, followed by Davy, and put into the ambulance.

'I think mum's getting sick,' I said. Aaron was looking out the window.

Sharon opened the door then. 'Mummy has had her baby and has to go to the hospital,' she told us. 'Now you two go downstairs while I clean up and don't come back up till I call ye, alright?'

As we passed the bathroom, the door swung out and inside

we saw blood and water on the floor, and towels thrown about everywhere. I didn't know where babies came from, so I didn't put two and two together. And I don't remember being too worried after I heard about the baby.

I was delighted with my new sister. When we were brought to the hospital, I remember my mum looking really sick and very tired. The baby was tiny, and due to her premature birth she developed pneumonia. She recovered but was always a sickly baby.

There were other babies after that. Davy never got the son he wanted, but I got four beautiful sisters: Lorraine, Catherine, Victoria and then little Jamiee-Leigh. Aaron was there too, the big brother, although he was away from home as soon as possible.

We will always be connected in our family ... those of us who are left, that is. Those of us who hung on and made it through the darkness that came after Davy Tweed set his sights on you.

3

Merry Christmas?

When I was five, my dad sent me a parcel by post from where he was living in the UK. This had become routine since he left. My mum would leave our parcel where we could see it when we came in from school. We learned to expect them for our birthdays and Christmas, and that was pretty much the only contact we had with our dad.

Inside the parcel that arrived for my fifth birthday was a Magic Moves Barbie. I had a collection of Barbies by this point, but this one was special – she came in a pink and silver box wearing a mint-green dress and a cloak embellished with white fur. Her arms moved on their own, at the push of a switch. I'd been seeing the ad for Magic Moves Barbie for months, where other little girls played with her, pressing her button to make her arms go up and down, and I had wished so much that she was my doll. Now she was.

A few days after she arrived, I went to play with a new friend I had made in the estate, down the bottom end. It is funny driving by that cul-de-sac now, as an adult, and seeing how small it is, because as a child it felt huge. I kept my dolls in an old leather bag that a neighbour from our old house had given me. I kept everything I owned in that bag. I dragged it around until I found a suitable spot to unzip it, untangling one Barbie from another as I lifted them out to play. I brought the whole bag with me to this new girl's house.

'Look what I've got,' I said. I wanted to impress her.

I'm not sure I did impress her though, as I lifted one Barbie after another out of that bag and she sat with one old one in her hands, with no change of outfit, no shoes and matted hair. She put her doll down.

'Play w' mine,' I said and after a pause she did, swapping one for another, changing clothes and using the small plastic brushes to pull their hair.

'Hey Amanda,' her mum said around the door of the shed we were playing in, 'we're gonna have lunch now.' She cast her eye over the Barbies. 'Go up home now for a bit sure you can come back after.'

I left the Barbies there, on the floor of the shed, and ran home, where my mum was waiting with my lunch too.

'Now,' she said, 'sit down there and eat that.'

After I was done, I ran back down the road, only to find the shed closed and locked.

I knocked on the door and said to the little girl, 'My Barbies are in your shed.'

She crossed her arms. 'My brother locked the shed up,' she said.

My heart sank. 'But my Barbies are in there,' I said.

'Well, I don't know where the key is,' she said.

I ran all the way home in tears, telling my mum the story as soon as I got in the door. I expected her to put on her coat and go down with me, but she didn't. A woman who lives in fear of conflict doesn't go looking for it, I suppose. She sympathised and said it was terrible, but I think she thought, as I did, that the brother would come back and the shed would be opened and I could get them then. So I tried to be patient, but the shed stayed locked and the key lost no matter how many days I called in to see.

Then one day I called in and it was clear that they had moved out. When the new occupier moved in I ran down, convinced he would have my Barbies, innocently thinking they would still be there. Of course, they were not. The man opened the shed and showed me – it was empty. He told me it was empty when he moved in.

The following Christmas, I remember we had a small plastic tree that was decorated all over with silk-covered baubles, ones where the individual threads were wound around and around the ball until they were covered. Some of them had gold or jewels stuck onto them with glue. We had tinsel and coloured lights as well, and there was a tiny angel dressed in red on the top of the tree. In advance of the big day, we put the presents on the floor underneath the tree and my mum hung the cards we'd got from our school friends on a string up the banister. I don't think I was ever so excited for Santa as I was that year, in the prime of my childhood.

My mum's brothers, Uncle Ken and Uncle Adam had come over the night before Christmas Eve – maybe to drop presents – and then gone out for a drink in the local pub, where they ran into Davy. Later, Uncle Ken came back up to our house again, leaving the other two in the pub, and ended up falling asleep on the couch.

When Davy came home, drink-fuelled, instead of turning on my mum as he usually would, he turned on Uncle Ken, asleep on the couch, and started to pull him across the floor and punch him. My mum attempted to stop Davy and got pushed out of the room. Then Davy grabbed my uncle around the neck and dragged him out the door, throwing him into the street. He shut the door behind him, caught his breath and turned his attention to my mum.

The commotion caught the attention of the neighbours and someone called the police, who were in the area and pulled up outside soon after. When Davy saw the flashing blue against the closed curtains, he pressed my mother up against the wall with a hand to her throat and hissed, 'If you say one word I will kill you, right?'

She promised she wouldn't tell. But she didn't need to, her bruised and bloodied face telling the police exactly the story of what was going on in our house. But – as was often the case – the police looked at my mum and her husband and chalked it up to 'a domestic'. In our culture, women sometimes need chastising, wives sometimes deserve a beating, it would seem.

The police went back down the path and got into their car, despite knowing that men can kill women with their bare hands, despite knowing that a punch from a man can kill a woman instantly. Despite the fact that Davy Tweed was six foot six and nearly twenty stone, while my mum was tiny and weighed nothing. They left anyway. They didn't even make a note of it.

When we went downstairs on Christmas Eve morning, the presents were smashed, and the paper torn and kicked around. The tree had fallen over, the cards and decorations had been pulled down, and there were what looked like pools of porridge around the hall and sitting room. Uncle Adam, who had been at the pub past closing, was asleep on the couch and I thought he had done the damage. I was so mad at him. Didn't he know Santa was coming tonight?

My mum came down, hearing us moving around.

'Don't be minding that,' she said. Holding one arm across her stomach, she used the other to move things and clean up.

I found out years later that the 'porridge' was where Davy had punched my mother so badly she had vomited. That's how hard he hit his wife.

It was the way back then that people picked up the makings of dinner on Christmas Eve, but my mother didn't make it to the butcher and to the grocer to do that. She had been beaten too badly to think of going out. She could barely move around the house let alone around the town. When she moved she winced, and she shuffled from place to place to get the house ready for the next day as best she could.

I went to bed that night thinking there was no way Santa was going to come. Perhaps it was the thought that my mum and Santa spoke to each other, perhaps it was the belief that Santa didn't come to houses where people were bad. I remember praying in my bed, clasping my little hands together as hard as I could and squeezing my eyes shut in dedication as I whispered a plea to God that Davy would leave my mum alone. I chanted it under my breath, and then tagged on at the end that it would be good if he could have a word with Santa to make sure he could come. My teacher had told me that you could ask God for favours, and I knew from the songs we sang every day at assembly that God was the one who had all the power. Either way, this was all I could do. Prayer was my only power. I was five years old.

When I woke the next morning, I remembered my prayer. But nothing seemed different, so I didn't wake my brother, I just took the stairs down to the living room to see if Santa had got my message. The door was slightly open and I saw the lights on the tree were on, the curtains were drawn and the room was tidy.

Santa always left us fruit in cut-up stockings made from old tights cut off at the knee and hung from the mantelpiece – all sorts, mandarins, red and green apples, and a pear if we were lucky. We got a new outfit under the tree every year; this year, for me, it was a red tartan dress with a black bow around the neck. I also got roller boots and a Barbie. I was glad of the Barbie but still bitter over my lost ones. The boots were blue leather with a yellow and red stripe on them across the heels. The wheels were a bright neon yellow and I thought there was nothing in the world like those roller boots. Aaron got a skateboard with sandpaper on its top side, a graffiti swirl underneath and big blue wheels.

Davy's mum, a traditional farmer's wife, came to the house not long after that to bring us some presents. I don't remember what they were now, but I remember when she set her eyes on my poor mother, looking like a second-place boxer, she pulled her in and held her really tight. She decided then and there to take myself and Aaron to her house, to 'give you two a chance to sort the row out,' she said to my mum.

I didn't want to go, not at all, but I was ordered to pick one of the toys I had got and to put my shoes on.

'I don't want to go to the farm,' I said, trying not to cry. I wanted to stay and use my new roller boots. But I did what I was told, picked up the new Barbie and left my skates there for later.

'You'll have a lovely dinner,' my mother said, and I think she was relieved we would be fed, but her eyes filled with tears and she found it hard to get the words out as she said goodbye. Not spending Christmas with her kids was further punishment she didn't deserve.

It was around then my nightmares started ... the ones where I would wake under a dead weight, unable to move or cry out.

Not long after that my mum noticed blood in my underwear.

4

Fear Turns to Terror

My mother tells me that she told Davy when she found the blood in my underwear and he reached out to his sister, who was a nurse, in concern. That bothers me, because it's so manipulative, given that, of all the adults in my life, he knew what the medical issue was. When his sister raised safeguarding concerns and asked my mum if any men could be interfering with me, Davy focused the attention on a man across the road, a harmless man with an intellectual disability, who often gave us sweets when we were playing outside.

We called that man 'Crutchie', because he walked with a crutch, and the sweets he offered us were never the kind we wanted. Humbugs, clove rocks and sweets in foil wrappers.

'Was somebody touching you down there, Mo?' my mother asked me after Davy's sister left. She called me 'Mo' like most people did, deeming Amanda too grown-up for the curly-haired, baby-faced child I was. She used diminutives for all of her children.

'Was it that weirdo across the road?' Davy asked me, and he pointed out the window with a wagging finger.

'If I see more of it in her underwear I will be going to the doctor,' my mum said to Davy. 'Has anyone done something to you Mo?' she asked me.

'Nobody did it,' I said, not making connections with my nightmares and the physical state I was in. I wanted the questions to stop because Davy was getting wound up. My mum was in danger when he was in a mood.

One day, I was playing out in the fields with my friends and having the most satisfying time. It was one of those perfect days when everyone was out and the games were great. A while later, I heard Davy calling me loudly, and saw him standing on the road beckoning me back.

I knew I was in trouble. He never called us.

'Go up to your room,' he barked at me.

I remember sitting on my bed really trying to figure out what I had done wrong, running the day through my head. The bed I sat on was made, my dolls were put away, the meals I had been given I had eaten, I hadn't made a mess.

Davy came in through the door of my bedroom and closed it behind him. He leaned his weight on it.

'Do you have something you want to tell me, Amanda?' he said.

I pressed my hands into the mattress. What could this be about?

'I don't know,' I said.

'Did you go to the toilet outside, Amanda?' he asked me. His voice was low and cold.

My cheeks went hot. I had. I'd held it for ages because we were in the middle of such a good game and home seemed so far, so I'd gone behind a bush like I'd seen the boys do many times. How did he know that? How did he see me? Anyway, what was the big

27

deal? I'd had to wee outside before when we were out at the park and there was nowhere for me to go. Wasn't this the same thing?

'I did go,' I said.

He reached down, grabbed me up off my bed and then he sat down and pulled me across his knee, face down, so my head was practically on the floor and my legs were swinging.

'You won't be sitting down for a week,' he said, 'not when I'm finished with you.'

And with that he pulled my trousers and my pants down and exposed my bare bottom. I was horrified and embarrassed, but those emotions were quickly replaced with terror as he swung his hand away and landed it back with huge force against my bare skin with a slap. The sting ricocheted through my body, the force of it went through my bones. I cried out, in a scream, but before I could inhale, he knocked the last bit of air out of me with another whack.

'Stop making noise or I'll keep going,' he said.

But I screamed again and he slapped again. Harder and harder, over and over, until I was numb and in shock and I didn't scream. I could barely breathe. He let go of my arm and let me slide off his knee onto the carpet with my trousers and pants down.

'If you ever do that again that's what you'll get,' he spat and pushed himself up to standing with his hands, dusted himself down, coughed to get his own breath back from the exertion of the beating, and left the room. The door stayed open.

I rolled over and attempted to stand up, but my trousers were caught around my knees, so I pulled them up. It really hurt. I lay there, face wet, lungs heaving, in so much pain. My bottom was burning, the skin bruised and aching from the force of his hand.

I went from being afraid of Davy to being absolutely terrified of him. I was not a child who was used to being corporally punished. A few soft taps on the hand or legs by my mother was all I had experienced till then.

I had feared being shouted at by Davy since we met him, and I had practised being as good as possible around him because I knew that if he started shouting at us it was likely that my mother would be beaten later. I had learned to cry silently, knowing that the sound of my wails would enrage Davy. 'You were all picture and no sound,' my mother would say when we talked about that years later.

It was a survival technique. I wanted to protect myself, but I think more than that I was trying to protect my mum. My whole childhood was spent with a mother who was bruised and battered, with black eyes and bust lips. I felt like those injuries were my fault – a deep sense of responsibility I've yet to fully shake. As a child I did not know how to speak about it, so I would think about it. My mum would always tell us not to worry about it, that she just fell over, even though she knew I had seen the violence with my own eyes.

It was a strange state of denial we all lived in. If my mum got battered, I would find something I did to explain it. I'd decide it was the doll I left on the chair, or the curtains I didn't pull. Even if there was nothing, I would find something. I never told my mum it was my fault because I didn't want her to blame me and hate me for the punishments she was taking that I deserved. I kept my suffering to myself. So we never spoke much about our pain, and that was – in so many ways – our downfall.

Davy didn't get away scot-free, not all the time. There was one time he made the mistake of going after my mother when she ran out of the house. He caught up with her and grabbed her by the hair, pulling so hard that he ripped chunks of it out at the root. Then he dragged her back to the house by it, as she struggled and clutched at her head and held onto his wrists to try to get to her feet.

Unnoticed by Davy in his rage, he had been seen by a couple of the husbands from the estate, who came around the corner, and they had decided to call up a gang of men to have a word with Davy about his treatment of his wife.

Later that evening two men came to the house and knocked on the door. Davy answered it.

'Davy can you step out for a bit?' one of them asked. Davy looked up the street where there was a large gang waiting.

'I'll be out in a minute,' he said and shut the door.

The mood of the house went instantly cold, as if a film of ice had formed over everything, and Davy began to pull drawers open, taking knives out and tucking them into the band of his trousers. He took his pellet gun from above the fridge where it was kept and grabbed my brother's baseball bat before leaving the house.

My mum saw the crowd of men, so she followed him out and shuffled after him, trying to protect him even though he had just badly beaten her. The men circled Davy, like wolves around a large animal. Davy went for one of them, and the circle exploded in pushing and shoving. Someone struck Davy in the face and he staggered.

'Stop it!' my mum shouted at them. 'All of you against him, it's not right.'

The men ignored her and continued pushing and shoving Davy.

'Get back to the house now,' he roared, sending her back home.

Aaron and I were trying to watch from his bedroom, but we couldn't really see.

Men were gathering, spilling out onto the road. We heard shouts and arguments, nothing, and then more shouts. Then we heard someone yell, 'He has a gun!' Things got really wild and people started coming out of their houses to see the commotion.

Uncle Danny ran in. 'There's a riot and Davy is in it,' he said, out of breath.

'I know,' my mum said, 'there's too many against him.'

We heard the sounds of police cars and my mum let out a sigh of relief. A few moments later Davy came in. He had thrown the gun away somewhere.

The police came to the door and asked him if he had a gun. He said he had no gun, then they asked him for the bat and he gave it to them and they went away. We were sent straight to bed and that was the end of it.

5

Cherry Gardens

My mum tried to run away with us a few times. I remember one time, after a particularly bad row, when Davy had left her so badly injured that she could barely move, her father came down in his van and helped her pack us all up and took us away to Belfast. Aaron and I sat in the back of the van, on top of bags of clothes and bedding, having a great time pretending we were in a rocket ship in space. Mum sat in the front with the baby, quiet.

Our break for freedom was short-lived. Davy came to my grandparents' house that night and threatened to smash the windows if we didn't get in his car.

Sometimes Davy would throw my mum out, pushing her out the door and closing it behind her. We were his hostages then, and my mother would bang at the door begging to get back in. Davy told my mum time and time over that she was a bad mother, that she was crazy. He told her that if she tried to leave him the courts would award us children to him and he would make our lives a misery. My mum was a really good mother, but she was depressed, driven demented by life in a pressure cooker, always on her guard, being pummelled and pinned into a corner by the one person she should have been able to trust. She lived in hell.

She told me that once when he pushed her out of the house while we older ones were at school, the baby, Lorraine, cried so much that he opened the door and pushed her out of it too. My poor mum, stuck and isolated in Ballymoney, walked down to the train station with my sister and caught the train to Belfast. When they were walking up the road to her parents' house, she noticed Davy's car coming up the road and so she hid in a garden with Lorraine tucked under her coat. Poor little Lorraine started crying and my mum had to put her hand over the child's mouth.

This sounds like a scene from a thriller film where someone is being hunted by a bad guy ... it should never be someone's actual lived experience. But all too often, in the world of women, it is.

Davy spotted them in the garden and roared so loudly that Lorraine, newly out of nappies, wet herself with fright.

'Get into the car, Margaret,' he said, 'before I get out and drag you into it.'

My mum stayed where she was.

'Do you not get who I am, Margaret?' he said. 'I know a guy who would cut you up with a chainsaw. Do you not realise I can have that done anytime I want? And your kids too?'

She believed him. She went back.

No matter how many times she ran, no matter how many times he threw her out, in the end the pattern would repeat and repeat until we were all too worn down and battered to know how to dream of change at all. Eventually my mum stopped running.

Davy moved us back to the bungalow in Cherry Gardens. This was the same one we had lived in when he and my mum first got together – Rose had moved out and so his aunt sold it to him and it became our family home. We were given the freedom to decorate our rooms as we wished. I was sharing with my little sister in a bedroom off the living room. She was small, so I went to Walkers on the Main Street and chose a white paper with a ditzy floral print in pastel colours. My mum hung that paper herself, she was great at anything like that. We were given bunk beds, and I, of course, got the top. We also had wardrobes, drawers and a toy box.

In that estate a bread van would come every week on the same day at the same time and everyone would go out to line up to buy bread and the Veda malt loaf that he stocked. There wasn't a day that van pulled in that I wasn't excited to see it. I would always run like the clappers to be first in line. And when the bread man would see me coming, he would pull out the tray of chocolate and crisps, knowing that sometimes my mum would give in and let us have fresh bread sandwiches, buttered and filled with Tayto cheese and onion crisps, followed by some sweeties or chocolate. We never knew which would be the day she would give in to this idea, but it was often enough that sometimes I still remember it and my mouth will water and I will make a Tayto sandwich again – the combination never lets me down.

Where we lived in Cherry Gardens was in a wee cul-de-sac – two large squares of grass around each of which eight bungalows stood. On the edge of one set of bungalows, there was a lane up to a farm – still there now – and on the edge of the other set, a lane to the leisure centre, and there were huge open spaces around us, so for small children it really was a natural playground.

We loved playing on the 'green'. It was the meeting point for all the local children and we were lucky to live facing it. There was a bench in one corner. We never had to worry that there would be nobody out, not only because we had each other to play with but also because we could see the entire space from our door.

We would play football, chasing and 'Curby' – a game where you would face an opponent on an opposite curb and attempt to bounce the ball back against the curb to catch it yourself, but if they caught it, they would fire it at you, and if they hit you, they won. Or maybe that was just the excuse my brother gave to hit me with a ball and get away with it!

Playing outside was safe and real fun. The road ran around the green and there would be kids on bikes or go-carts racing around, and then we would play in the middle, making daisy chains or playing football. Our cousins would come up, and we would create elaborate games of make-believe. I remember after a family wedding, we played weddings on that green, finding wire to make rings and making bouquets from the local trees and bushes that were in bloom. Davy wasn't around, so my mum joined in, setting up the reception for us with juice and biscuits and providing a towel for the bride to wear as a veil.

The new house was close to school and we walked there each morning. I liked school, my headmaster and my teacher. And Davy wasn't there.

We learned how to skip in school. The older girls would swing a rope and everyone would line up and jump in, chanting, 'Mickey Mouse had a house, what number was it? One, two, three, four ...' I knew that number because my wallpaper in our first home in Belfast had Mickey Mouse with his house on it. I always felt so confident saying that number as I took the run into the ropes.

I wonder if all the little moments of joy as a child – the crisp sandwiches, the play weddings, the warmth and safety of our

mum when Davy was away, the lovely school and teachers –
I wonder if those things weighed out in a sort of balance, not
allowing the scales to tip. At that time I lived through pockets of
hell, dark cruel places that would swallow me up, but then my
real life, my child's life, would lift me back out and let me go on
and grow.

Later, as I became more aware of everything that was wrong
with this picture, the scales did tip, sending me sliding down the
deep banks of darkness.

My new bedroom opened into the living room and I would have
to cross that room to get to the bathroom.

One night I woke and needed to wee, so I got up. Once I
cracked the door, as I always did to check if someone was still
up, I noticed the room was dark, but the TV was on. I hoped it
was Uncle Danny watching – he was always in our house – but
then I noticed it was Davy and he was sitting in his dressing gown
watching the screen. I made a little run past him to the bathroom,
my head down.

On the way back through the living room I tried to dart past
again, but he called to me.

'What are you doing awake?' he said.

'I just needed the toilet,' I said.

'I'm going to work shortly,' he said, 'just watching the TV ...'
He pointed at it and I looked. On the screen I saw a naked woman
and a man wearing just a shirt and no trousers at all standing in
a stairwell. I didn't know what to do. I knew seeing adults' naked
bodies was not good, it wasn't something I should watch. So I
tried to go into my room, but Davy called me back.

'Can you do me a favour, honey?' he said. 'Would you mind keeping an eye if I have a nap here, and wake me for work so I won't miss my shift?'

He always called me 'honey'. To this day that word turns my stomach.

I looked back into my room.

'You can go back to bed after,' he said, 'just keep an eye on me and wake me for work, won't you?'

Something felt really off about all of it, but I agreed. He asked me to sit on the chair, and he got down on the floor and lay down with his head on a cushion in front of me. His feet reached the TV.

I stared at the digital clock. The couple on the television were frightening me, as they were both fully naked now and doing strange things. The woman was sitting on a kitchen worktop and making noises I didn't like.

I stared at the clock. I felt like I needed the toilet again.

I counted down with the clock, ten minutes.

I looked at Davy. He seemed fast asleep. Then he rolled over with a heavy sigh and his head came up and rested on the chair beside me. I pulled my legs up under me and shifted back in the seat.

Davy made another loud sigh and grabbed one of my legs. I looked at his eyes and they were shut.

'Wake up, Daddy,' I said.

He rolled over again. Now he was face down on my leg, and his other hand slid up and grabbed my other leg. He pulled me so my legs were pinned by his shoulders, and then he pushed me down and moved the gusset of my underwear over and assaulted me.

I hit Davy on the head, I said stop over and over, but I kept my cries stifled because I didn't want to wake anyone else. I believed Davy was asleep and these awful things were happening to me by mistake.

Suddenly Davy sat up with his face turned away. He yawned and stretched and turned back to me as if in surprise.

'Why are you crying? What happened?' he said.

I just picked myself up and ran back to the bathroom. I did not know what had happened, why Davy had done that to me in his sleep. I curled up on the mat in the bathroom, holding in long hard sobs, refusing to let my grief come to the surface. I wanted this to be a nightmare, but I knew it was not. I wanted my mother, but I knew I had to let her sleep. I thought I would stay in that bathroom forever because I could not go back out there to see Davy. Then I heard him opening the hall door and I heard his creaking steps. He knocked on the bathroom door.

'Are you okay in there?' he said in a low voice. I got up and stood staring at the door.

'I'll come out in a minute,' I said. I started the water and washed my hands.

'I need to use the bathroom,' he said.

My stomach twisted and churned so hard, it felt as though I was being strangled. I took my time.

I opened the door and walked out, attempting to ignore him and just get to my room. He was back sitting on the sofa with his dressing gown open, showing his body off, exposing himself to the little child he had just sexually assaulted.

'Come here, Amanda,' he said.

I remember the quiet in that room when he said that. I could hear the teeth chattering in my head and I was shaking so much I was unbalanced. I didn't move closer, I stayed where I was.

Davy Tweed sat there naked and asked me, as if there was any question, to tell him what had happened when he was asleep. I didn't have words for that act, I didn't know what to say. I stumbled over words; I gestured and shook my head when it was simply impossible to explain what he had just done. I had no vocabulary for that. I was eight.

'Ah ... I think I mistook you for your mum,' he said.

I listened to that and my mind raced as to what that could mean. Why would he do what he did to me to my mum? I didn't know about sex. I just knew I had been hurt and scared and I didn't want this conversation. How could he think I was her when I was so small? People sometimes said I was my mum's image. Maybe that was it.

My childish thoughts were jumbled and then interrupted, as Davy started to cry. I felt sorry for him.

'See, Amanda,' Davy said, 'if you told anyone what I did by mistake, the police would send me to jail, and if that happened you and your mum and Aaron and the baby would all have to live on the street and you'd have nothing, no food or anything ...'

'I won't tell the police,' I said.

'You can't tell your mum either,' he said, 'promise?'

I stood there.

'If you told anyone, they'd take you away from your mum and put you and Aaron in a home.'

'You better not do it to me again,' I said, feeling a little power in front of this man with tears on his cheeks.

He snapped back, 'Sure you enjoyed it!' And I was instantly

hit with the wall of shame that still blocks me in. That was not true, but the way he said it was with such confidence. Then he grabbed me by the wrist.

'Show me your fanny,' he said pulling me back and forth by the wrist as I stood there. I shook my head.

'Just your pants then,' he said, and I shook my head again, so he pulled me right up to him, sitting there with his chest, belly and penis exposed. He pulled my nightie up, holding me with a hard grip I couldn't get out of and he began to masturbate. I closed my eyes tight.

'Open your eyes,' he ordered me, 'you're to watch me now.'

I stood there with my eyes open, watching this disgusting warped pig pleasuring himself in front of me, and if I turned my eyes or closed them, he would shake me by the arm, really hurting me, forcing me to return my attention to what he was doing. And when he was finished, he asked me if I knew what the white mess on his chest was.

'It's sperm,' he told me, when I said I didn't. He said it as casually as if it were a biology lesson. He released his grip and I ran back to my bed, curling up in the furthest corner and crying myself to sleep.

I wanted to run to my mum and wake her and tell her. But I didn't.

I wanted to tell on him the next morning as I sat chewing my breakfast, not able to swallow because my throat was so sore from crying. But I didn't.

I wanted to tell my mum as she said goodbye to me at the door and sent me off to school. But I didn't.

I wanted to tell the teachers, the people on the street, the police. But I didn't.

Davy himself had told me he would go to jail, so I knew what he had done was something so wrong, but I didn't tell anyone. Perhaps I didn't have the words to, or the skills to, or perhaps in my child's mind I thought my mum would be homeless, just as Davy had said. I took this burden on because I didn't know what it was. The silence and shame around child abuse became the greatest power Davy had over me.

After that first time, he abused me most nights.

6

Two Faces

'I want Davy to adopt me,' I said from the back seat of his car. We were on our way home from a rugby match in Belfast.

There was a silence at first. My mother was so surprised she turned fully around in her seat and stared at me. She knew I was scared of Davy, though she believed it was because of his violence towards her, and his threats.

'What's this about?' she said.

'I want to be the same as Lorraine,' I said.

Davy looked at me in the mirror. 'I'm not sure it's as easy as you think,' he said.

I looked deliberately sad. 'I want to be like Lorraine,' I said again.

You see, I had had a brainwave. I had the sudden idea that the reason Davy abused me was because I wasn't his flesh and blood. At that age I was not educated on where babies came from, but I knew enough that Davy couldn't turn into my daddy. But I became convinced that if Davy adopted me, the terrifying ordeals would cease.

I missed my own father. We never saw him, but we did get presents in the post on birthdays and at Christmas. And as we got older, he would send money in a card. He never forgot us.

We went over once to stay with him for a few weeks in the summer. We went by aeroplane from Belfast airport. I remember it so well, as I had badly bruised legs from a fall I had had out of a tractor trailer that was parked on our road. We had climbed up to play on the hay, and one of the girls from our road asked me to help her up. She ended up pulling me down by accident and I fell right onto both knees on the tarmac. I couldn't stand for ages after that and had to be helped home – my mum was genuinely worried that my knees were broken. But then, after a good rub, she knew they weren't and so I was put up in bed with paracetamol. The next day they were black and blue down to the shins.

My mum brought us up to the airport and came to the boarding gate. It wasn't as unusual then for children to fly alone. I don't remember much except the snack and drink we got on the plane, handed across to me in my window seat by a beautiful air hostess with red lipstick and her hair in a bun. On the other side, we were shown the way out and there was my dad and his new wife waiting for us.

When we got back to his house, he showed us where we would sleep, in a small room with a bed made up for my brother and a little pull-out trundle for me. I slept so well in that trundle bed. That summer in Matlock was one that felt like it lasted forever. The weather was good and we ran about in shorts and T-shirts. My dad put the effort in, years of outings and adventures piled into one summer. We went to theme parks and met cousins we had forgotten. We went to village fairs, the ones where there are farm animals all spruced up and stalls with jam tarts and scones for sale, and competitions like throwing a wellie. When we pulled up in the car park, my dad would turn to us as we sat in the back of his car and say, 'Now I mustn't forget to give you your pocket money.' Then he would hand us each a fifty pence piece. I would buy myself sweets with the pocket money; a striped paper bag stuffed with fudge and jellies. We went strawberry picking and filled tiny baskets with handles made of straw up to the top with big strawberries. A man weighed our collections at the end and we paid for them, and my dad's wife made us a dessert of fresh vanilla ice cream and chopped up strawberries after tea.

Right there, sitting at the table, my dad chatting away to my brother about football and other things, my stepmother carrying a big pot of tea to the table and patting me on the head in a motherly way, I wanted to shout, 'Let me stay!' But I didn't. The words crowded in my throat and made it burn, but I held them back. I did want to live there. It was lovely and calm and safe, but I could never leave my mother. At that tender age I believed that I needed to be there to somehow protect her. I had to go home.

Back home nothing had changed for me. Davy made up for lost time. So I had this lightbulb moment, and now there was a conversation about how I could be adopted.

'Maybe if you wanted, we could change your name to Amanda Tweed?' Mum said.

I thought about that.

'What would your own daddy think if you did that?' Mum said then.

I thought about that. Maybe we wouldn't have to tell him. My focus was on getting myself out of this predicament I was in, where Davy was doing things to me and making me do things to him. This plan I had would work, I knew it.

If I was a 'Tweed' that might mean he would treat me like my sister and leave me alone.

'I don't think Daddy minds,' I said. I was confident.

'What about you, Aaron?' Davy said.

Aaron stayed silent. It would take him a few days to agree. Once he did, the ball began rolling, our names were changed in school and eventually by deed poll.

But nothing changed at all.

My feelings of regret were almost instant, as soon as I first heard my new name over the roll call in assembly. People were referring to me as 'Davy Tweed's daughter' and that somehow made things more disgusting, more shameful. Not only that but expectations were put on me that I hadn't had before, like PE teachers expecting me to be sporty and signing me up for teams I didn't want to be on.

Our school had a popular group, as most schools do, and I wasn't part of it. My aim was never to be the peacock on any occasion – I kept a low profile, kept myself to myself. I preferred to be seen as 'one of the boys', deeming myself unattractive and unwanted.

'I've a thick skin,' I would tell everyone, with my outside face on, hoping they would believe me. I laughed at jokes made at my expense, stayed away from forming female relationships and stuck to the knowledge that my cousins and sisters loved me and would never reject me like these girls could. When they pushed me, jealous perhaps of my cordial friendships with the objects of their affections, I pushed back harder.

Then I would go home and replay the cruel things they said in my head, and I believed every single word of it.

Most nights I would wake to that tall shadow looming over me, and he would grope and molest me as I lay on the top bunk. That's how large a man Davy Tweed was. He would creep into our room at night and assault me again and again as I lay there terrified and quiet as a mouse, because I didn't want to wake my sister for fear that he would turn his attention to her too.

I wanted to protect her. It was a strength I felt I had in this powerlessness. If I put up with this, she would never have to.

There were certain times when I was free of the abuse. He couldn't get me when I stayed at Granny's. And so I stayed there as much as I could – Halloween, Easter, Christmas. I would always have to be in my mother's house for the day itself, on Easter or Christmas, but the rest of the holidays, like the week between Christmas and New Years, would be in Granny's house. I stayed with Granny a lot as a child.

Holidays in my Granny's house in Belfast couldn't come fast enough – that relief once I would get through her door, the feel of the small bed she made up for me that I would climb into knowing nobody was going to come into the room at night to hurt me.

When I stayed there, where I slept depended on who else was staying. If my uncles were there, I would be in the box room, on the little bed with a little white duvet folded up over a flat sheet and tucked under the mattress. If there was no one else in the house, I could sleep in the big room with its orange wardrobe on which the door slid back and forth. If my cousin Jessica was staying too, we would share the bed and play in there. There was a bag of perfumes in the wardrobe, which Granny never wore – she got a lot of it given to her at Christmas. The bag was bulging out with all the packets and bottles, and we would try various scents on. One of them was called Tweed, and Jessica and I thought that was funny.

Granny would tell me to go to bed when my day was done, and I would happily go. The room was made up for me, the door was ajar and would stay that way. Nobody was coming to get me there.

But at home I was on my guard. Davy had a routine. He worked shifts, so it was easy for him to come in and wake me late into the early hours while my mother slept. I constantly worried he might come into the bedroom if I had friends sleeping over, so I always suggested sleeping at their house instead, knowing that he couldn't prey on them there.

When I was around nine, one of the local schools shut down and many of their students came to our school instead. One of the new girls and I became firm friends and, as was the way, we would ask for sleepovers at least once a month and would take turns. In my house I would be on edge and distracted, not able to fully immerse myself in play with her.

'Your house is a bit boring,' she said to me one day.

'I don't mind if we only ever stay at your house,' I said.

Her house was out in the country and she had a family that, to my childish eyes, looked like the perfect one. A tall dad and older brothers, a sweet mum and her, the baby. They always had days out together and when I was staying over, they would take me with them. I loved them for that, treating me like one of theirs all day, never singling me out at all. From them I knew what 'family' could look like.

In some ways, strangely, I had something in common with Davy Tweed. At least I can see that now. He was living a life with two faces that he would switch on and off, and so was I. He was the monster in the home, the aggressive violent sexual predator who would leave the house, don a smile and make himself the world's hero. Outside the house, I was the girl who stood up for herself, the one who didn't give a shit, the bolshy bad girl. At home I was the other me, the real one, as real as Davy was at home where he showed his true self, the monster. I was the smallest hurt thing with no confidence, no strength and no self-worth at all.

We were the same but polar opposites. Both letting go of our outside personas as soon as the door closed behind us, both showing a face to the people of our community that was not our true face. Both avoiding the mirror because of what stared back at us. Both, perhaps, hating ourselves, but doing nothing to help it.

7

The Crash

If you have ever been in a car crash you will know what I mean when I say that time becomes still and everything moves like a slowed tape, in jolts.

I remember looking down at my sister, as our family car drove the long straight road from Belfast to Ballymoney where we lived, late at night, too late for children to be awake. And too dark and too wet for the slowed reactions of a drunk driver. As I moved a strand of hair from Lorraine's cheek, suddenly she was pushed back into me by an invisible force.

We had been staying in our aunt's house because Davy and my mum were away to a rugby match in Dublin. We had been dropped off on the Friday, with armfuls of duvets and pillows. Lorraine and I slept top and tail in the single room, and my brother was on the couch.

For some reason Mum and Davy arrived back on the Sunday night later than planned. Davy said he was tired and they decided to sleep at my aunt's for the night instead of packing us all into the car and going back up to Ballymoney. We all had to share that small single room and, since she was heavily pregnant, Mum was given the bed, tucking Lorraine in under the blankets with her, giving Davy his share of the floor beside me.

'I can sleep down with Aaron,' I said, standing in my nightdress beside the door. Everyone was fixing the coverings and placing pillows.

'Lie down here,' Davy said and patted the floor beside him.

'I can go down and sleep on the chair,' I said.

Davy patted the floor harder. 'Lie down, now.'

I didn't know how to argue my case. I didn't want to get in trouble and I didn't want to cause trouble. I lay down. I crossed my fingers, I hoped he would just lie there. My mum was so close. There was no way.

I lay there frozen and so did Davy; then I saw him lift his head up as if he was looking at my mum. She was still, one arm thrown over Lorraine, her breathing slow and rhythmic. She was asleep.

Davy reached across and grabbed my nightie, pulling me close into him. I slid across the floor with a whoosh. I could smell alcohol on his breath. He must have had a few pints in the pub after the game and ordered his pregnant wife to drive back to Belfast.

I don't know what was wrong with Davy. Something was. I'm sure people who have studied paedophilia have the answers, but I have no interest. Those things, like acts done to them in the past or a warped mind, are explanations, not excuses. Adults know what is right and what is wrong. He knew what was right and wrong too, because he kept his wrongs secret.

I could feel Davy's erect penis on my leg and he rubbed it against me. I nudged him with my elbow, but he didn't stop. So I pretended I was asleep and thrashed about as if I was having a nightmare, thinking that it might wake my mother. If she woke, she might take me into the single bed too.

Davy stopped, but only long enough to check my mum was still sleeping before he continued his usual routine of groping and molesting me.

I could not allow this.

I rolled away and stood up.

'Mum, Mum,' I said loudly enough that my mum opened her eyes.

'What is it, Amanda?' She was exhausted from the drive.

'I have a pain,' I said.

'Where is it, Mo?' she asked.

'It's in my … tummy.' I thought on the spot. 'I feel sick.'

Davy lay still, eyes closed.

'Don't wake your daddy,' my mum said. 'Go on downstairs and get yourself some water and I'll come down now too.'

When she said that Davy sat bolt upright.

'Let's go home,' he said.

'Home?' My mum was confused. 'There is no need, Davy.'

'If the child is sick, she needs her own bed,' he said. 'Let's just get in the car.'

And so we woke Lorraine, gathered up everything and went downstairs. My mum woke Aaron and we went out into the cold wet night and got into the car. It was so late, we were all so tired and Davy was driving with drink in him.

Lorraine lay across the two of us, Aaron and me, wrapped in a duvet with just her face out in the air, her head on my lap and her feet on his. I remember fixing a wee strand of her hair out of her closed eyes when suddenly she lifted off my lap, floating up in slow motion with the force of a fast car braking suddenly. There was a lull, then a screech that lasted for so long.

'Fuck, shit,' Davy said and his hands went white on the wheel and he turned it hard. Lorraine was pushed into me with the force of it and I was slammed into the back of the seat. I tried to hold on to her, but the duvet she was wrapped in had little grip.

It seemed like we went and went, the car spinning like a waltzer at the fair, all of us pushed to one side. Aaron slid across the seat and his full weight was on me, squashing me against the side of the car. Lorraine was in the space between our legs and the backs of the front seats, her eyes open and her mouth was forming a soundless O.

We flew across the road for what seemed like minutes, but of course it was only seconds, until we hit the other car with a bang. Everyone in the car flew forward.

The seatbelt guide, where the belt retracts, was pulled so hard with the weight of Davy, that it snapped the plastic side panel and as I came forward, airborne, the jagged edge of it sliced through my eyebrow like a knife. Immediately my vision was obscured with thick blood that poured out of the wound.

The car came to a stop and there was nothing but the sound of the engine. Davy kicked the smashed windscreen out and left the vehicle that way, without so much as a look in his wife's direction. There she was, probably seven months pregnant, after a bad crash, and he didn't so much as glance at her. But I did. I stared at the back of her seat until I saw her head turn and her face appear over the side. She winced, either from her own pain or the sight of her children's injuries. I looked at Lorraine. She was wedged in the well between the seats and was fine. She wiggled out of her duvet and sat up. When she looked at me, she screamed and climbed up onto the far side of the seat. I looked at Aaron. His chin was torn open, and bleeding. Pieces of glass and plastic littered the car.

'Are you feeling alright, Amanda?' my mum said.

I said I felt woozy, so she started having a conversation with me where I had to answer her back and forth.

'Stay awake, okay?' she said.

A man appeared at the side of the car and opened the door. They took my mum out, then us, and took us to the closest house to where the crash was. None of us knew where Davy had gone, but there were shouts and roars. When we went into that house and I looked down and saw my nightdress soaked through with blood, my first thought was not to make a mess. The carpets under my feet were cream and fluffy and I hesitated at the door – I didn't want to ruin them. But they took my hand and brought me into the kitchen and tried to get me to drink something sweet, maybe it was 7up. As soon as we had a minute to think, I felt deep guilt, so deep it hurt through my bones. I had stopped Davy and that was why he had made us leave. This was my fault.

'Can I go to the toilet?' I asked the room. A lady showed me the way.

The bathroom was wall-to-wall mirrors and I saw reflected back at me a horror scene, a ghost or vampire covered in blood. It was me. When I realised that I threw up.

The lady who had shown me the way came in and tried to help me clean myself up, but I was dazed and there was so much blood it was an impossible task. She fetched a paramedic, and they took my pulse and blood pressure. The lady held a compress to my wound.

'Have you any pains love?' the paramedic asked me.

'My tummy is sore,' I said, and he pressed on it and decided to send me to hospital in the ambulance. They sent mum in an ambulance on her own, and Aaron and me in another. Lorraine was supposed to come with us, but she was screaming blue murder, terrified and refusing to get in, so the people who had helped us offered to bring her in the car.

I don't think I realised how much worry my mum had at that moment. Being a mum myself now, I can't imagine seeing your kids in that way and also knowing that a seat belt had squeezed your pregnant belly, so the baby in your womb could be hurt too. In the hospital they checked the baby's heart rate and fluid levels and monitored Mum for shock-induced labour.

A nurse washed me. It was such a good feeling to get rid of the sticky blood that had matted my hair to my face. I wanted to tell her it was my fault, the accident. But a doctor came in and asked me what day it was, what school I was at, who my teachers were.

'I've a test in the morning,' I said, and he laughed when I said that.

'I don't think you need to worry about going to school tomorrow,' he told me.

I was stitched up and they let me lie down for a while on a hospital bed. Then the same doctor came in and asked me the questions he had asked before. I remember thinking, *this guy has lost his marbles*.

'Davy has to stay here for the night,' my mum told me when we were finally discharged. 'They need to monitor his heart.'

I remember hoping he would die.

My mum went back to the hospital the next day because of the pain, and we went to stay with Davy's sister up the road. She washed me again in a hot bath to get the remnants of blood out of my hair, and she put me up on her bed with the electric blanket on and a soft duvet, thick socks and a dressing gown over my pyjamas, but I still struggled to get warm.

Davy was discharged a few days later, much to my disappointment. It turned out my mother had fractured her spine. She was in so much pain, and each wince was like a lash to my guilty heart.

8

A Violent Man

Two babies were born in our family in the year after that crash. Our own baby, Catherine, who everyone was totally delighted with and my little cousin Gemma, daughter to Uncle Danny and his new wife. I had been a bridesmaid at their wedding, which had been on my birthday. They'd given me a day off school that day – I had been thrilled.

Catherine was in my care a lot of the time, mostly because my mum's fractured back took so long to heal and she couldn't carry baby baths or do much bending and lifting. I didn't mind, I loved babies, and Catherine – at least until she was in her terrible twos – was a wee dote. We were a good team, me and my mum, and of course Lorraine when she wasn't being more of a hindrance than a help in her enthusiasm to give a hand.

It's funny, because from the outside we really looked like a family should. My mum would stand in the tunnel at the end of rugby matches and run onto the pitch with one of us by the hand and one in her arms, who she would hand to Davy as he came off the field – the perfect family man. Who knew that behind closed doors he was slamming his fist into her soft stomach and kicking her as she lay on the floor desperately trying to crawl away from him? When he took one of us in his arms and waved at the singing crowd after a win, who would have seen that picture and thought it was possible that in the dead of night he was creeping across the floors of our landing and into my room to molest and hurt me in such cruel ways? When people looked across the clubhouse and saw us sitting together, us with our crisps and bottles of Fanta, Davy with his pint and my mum with a Diet Coke or, if she wasn't pregnant, a hot whiskey, who on earth would have concluded that this was a scene of hostages and their taker? Who knew that after nearly every match my mum would drive home and end the day with a serious hiding?

Nobody knew our secrets. But I did.

I remember once we were sent to Davy's parents for the day, up at the farm. Davy's father was a recent amputee, after a diabetic infection in his toe, and so was sitting in a high-backed recliner right up against the TV. We kids were sitting in a line on the sofa waiting to go home when we heard the gates open and the car outside. Granny Tweed had started to pack up our things when Davy came through the doors of the house shoving my mum in front of him. She fell face-first onto the sofa. She told me years later that just before that he had taken her out into the middle of nowhere after beating her black and blue and showed her where he would bury her when he killed her. He pushed her down onto the cold ground out there and started to strangle her, then stopped and beat her up instead.

'Davy!' Granny Tweed's face went really still, like she had turned all her expressions off. Davy ignored her and started berating my mum, who now sat on the floor. He then grabbed her by the material of her jacket sleeve and pulled her up. But she slipped out of the coat back onto the floor.

'Get up, stand up,' Davy said pulling on her arm again.

Granda Tweed attempted to look around the chair back, but he couldn't see so he raised his voice at Davy and told him to calm down.

'You're frightening the children,' he said, unable to do more than twist a fraction to the side. His chair was turned away from my mother, who was crawling towards the kitchen. She had blood on her face.

Davy stood there.

'Get into the kitchen all of you,' Granny Tweed said. In her hands she was twisting and untwisting the tea towel she had been using.

We went into the kitchen. There were tracks of tears in the blood on my mother's face.

'Wash your face,' Davy spat, 'you're making a show of me.'

She washed it a little at the sink, still out of breath, still crying, and then we got into the car and drove home in total silence except for the hitch in my mother's breathing.

As we pulled in to our driveway, Davy ordered us straight to bed. Then we had to endure the sounds of our mum being dragged up and down the house, the sounds of slaps and her pleas, the sounds of punches sending her flying into the thin walls. She ran down the hall and he followed her, a clear difference in the sounds of those two sets of footsteps, and then he threw her through our bedroom door with so much force she fell into the wardrobe.

He walked in after her, his chest heaving, his shoulders back. He was such a fit man, it took a lot to get him out of breath, but he was, pulling air in and letting it out like he had just run a mile.

'Don't youse start crying,' he said to us, 'she deserves everything she gets, don't you, Margaret?'

'Davy ...' my mum was really sobbing and his name came out with a wince, 'please don't ...'

'Don't what?' Davy stood over her, reached down and took her by the scruff of the neck and shook her like she was a bold dog. 'Now tell your children that you deserved this beating.'

My mum looked up at us and tried to smile. 'I deserved the beating ... don't worry, I deserved it,' she said.

I knew that was a lie. There was no badness in my mother. What I saw was a vulnerable, worn-out woman on the floor of my bedroom, and I was trapped into watching her suffer because I was a child. I had no idea about what true power was – I didn't know Davy was actually a weakling. I believed he was the most powerful person in the world, someone who could take life away. I didn't want to put my mum in any more danger. I'd already caused a car crash – I believed that.

The adult woman I am now wishes I could go back and kick in the door of that house and show Davy what actual power looks like. He was nothing more than a violent paedophile.

As time went on Davy stopped apologising to my mother when he battered her. She could do nothing right. Neither could any of us.

'Are you stupid?' He would say to my sisters when they struggled with their homework, nothing but little children trying to understand numbers and letters. He would shout at and berate them, 'You must be retarded.'

So we believed that about ourselves and those words followed us into school, where we feared getting things wrong and therefore didn't partake like we should have.

'Are you having another biscuit?' That was the way he pushed me down, that was what he chose to instil in me, the idea that I was fat. I have a round face and so I suppose it came easy to him, but the comments were constant. After a while I stopped enjoying food. He would make the sound effect of stomping feet when I'd walk in the room, or if I stood up he would act like I was filling the whole room. And when you do that to a child, not only do they start to believe it, but being bullied like that makes you do what you can to stop it. If I wasn't fat he couldn't say these things, he couldn't single me out.

So I stopped eating.

Starving yourself isn't an easy thing to do. But it gives you a great sense of power. When everything else is chaos, to have one thing fully under control is a calming force. For me, I couldn't control what was being done to my body by Davy, but I could control what went into it.

After the first few times that Davy commented on my weight or made sly remarks about me eating, I started weighing myself. I saw the numbers on the scale as something I could focus on, each time I lost a pound I felt victory over my life. And victory over Davy in some ways.

I lied about eating, skipping lunch in school, pretending I was eating in friends' houses, existing on a diet of Fanta and cups of tea. I thought chewing gum would fool my body into thinking I was eating, so I chewed gum all day. Friends told me I looked 'skinny' and I liked the feeling of accomplishment – it was satisfying.

I was always cold, always weak and my entire body ached all the time.

I shared a room with my sisters. There were three of us in there, with one single bed and a set of bunks. Davy would creep into that room when we were asleep and wake me up to molest me. By that stage I had stopped trying to avoid it, stopped trying to fight him off. There was no point, I never succeeded. I was resigned and I had decided to just get it over with.

One night he came into the room, drink-fuelled, and stood over my bed. He reached under the covers and used his other hand to masturbate as he stood there in the middle of the room.

'What are you doing, Daddy?' I heard my little sister Lorraine's voice from above me.

I have never felt like that before or since. Absolute terror for another person. My mind raced and I tried to predict what would happen. Davy turned slightly away and removed his hand from under my duvet. The hand he was using to masturbate fixed his trousers over his erection.

'I'm just saying goodnight to everyone,' he said in a cheery way. 'I've just come in to say goodnight ...'

He patted my bed, turned away from us and then around towards the door so his unzipped trousers wouldn't be noticed, and left the room. The light from the living room spread across the floor and disappeared as he opened and closed our door.

There was silence in the room, except for my hitched breathing. I wiped my tears with the back of my hand.

'Are you okay, Mo?' Lorraine asked.

'I'm okay, are you okay?' I said.

'Yes,' she said.

I put on the same cheery tone that Davy had. 'Alright, well go asleep, night night,' I said.

I worried all night. My thoughts raced around, never catching up to one another, one after the other. *Did she know? Did she see? Is she okay?*

I remember checking that Catherine was asleep, terrified that she had seen it too. I wondered if Lorraine had woken up before, and just how much she saw.

I felt such shame, and fear that she would be affected by it.

The next day she seemed okay, and I never mentioned it and neither did she.

Uncle Danny's new baby arrived eight months after Catherine. Gemma was a little gem and as they grew, she and Catherine became firm friends.

During the school term I helped out with Cat, but when school was finished for the summer I would spend more time in Belfast, taking all of my holidays up in Granny's, where I could run down to play with my cousin Jessica on the street just over. There was a wooded area there and we would swing from trees and explore, getting behind hedges and just sitting in there, or digging in the muck for treasure. I'd be between Granny's and Aunt Susan's every day, eating in either one, playing, resting. Aunt Susan took Granny shopping in the car and we would go too – life went at a slow pace and a safe pace. Nobody was ever quick to anger, there was never a calm before a storm, never bangs and cries coming from downstairs as I hid in my bed.

Uncle Ken still lived in Granny's and he was my godfather, and he used to bring me to the shop to spoil me with sweets. On the way down he would chat to me about things, ask how I was, and I loved it. I could relax.

It felt as though, over there in Belfast, I was free. My body was mine and it could do what it wanted. I used it to run and climb and dance, and at night I rested. When I woke up in Granny's, I always felt like myself, not some rat in a trap like I did at home. At home I felt like I was on death row, constantly waiting to be called to the executioner, begging him for mercy and never getting it. In Belfast I was truly on the other side of the wall, unfettered, a wild child, running about with my cousins, losing my breath from laughing.

Then one night Davy arrived at Granny's door saying he was too tired to drive back to Ballymoney, so she said he could stay there. He had never done that before. His compulsions had obviously got the better of him. That night he took my safe space away. From then on I was never again relaxed at Granny's – I would watch the door, flinching at every car that passed in case it would pull in.

Aaron left home as soon as he was seventeen. I didn't blame him. And it meant I got to move into his bedroom on my own. The small room that Aaron had been in was directly across from where my mother and Davy slept.

The abuse stopped. Night after night I would hear Davy's footsteps in the hall, but he never came into my room at all.

I used to lie awake waiting for it. I'd watch the door, like I always did when I was in my bunk. And when I fell asleep somewhere along the way I would wake now and again, with the creaks of the house or movement somewhere, and brace myself for his shadow across my bed. But he never came.

The last time he had abused me was that night when Lorraine woke up. I thought about her and Catherine, so vulnerable in their little room. I watched how Davy was around them, but I didn't know what I was looking for. Davy would sit his daughters up on his knee and I would watch their faces carefully for tells that they feared him in the same way I did.

They didn't seem different. I watched for it anyway.

9

A Step Too Far

A few years ago my mum told me about a time she ran away from Davy, pregnant and scared in a strange town in England that they were in for an event. During a beating in a hotel room where he tried to strangle her, she managed to get away from him and run. She made it to the airport and got a flight home with the intention of getting us kids and leaving him for good.

When she boarded the flight and as she was making her way down the aisle, she saw Davy's back – he had seemingly missed his own flight while looking for her. She spent that flight hiding low down in her seat and when they landed she stayed on board until everyone else had gone before leaving the aircraft.

Imagine being that terrified of the person you are living with. She told me she walked from the airport to her parents' house, about ten miles, and on the way, while looking over her shoulder, she spotted his car and hid in a garden until he passed.

I remember Davy arriving at the farm where we were being minded by his parents, and he announced as he came in the door that my mum wasn't coming back.

'Your mother is staying in England,' he said. I was fifteen years old, and I remember my heart stopped in my chest with the way he said it – I felt really deeply that Davy had killed my mother. I felt it all the way through my bones.

'Why?' someone asked.

'She missed her flight,' Davy said. 'You've to stay here for a bit longer.'

The phone rang then and Granny Tweed answered it. I heard her say, 'Hiya, Margaret,' and the relief flooded through me with such a rush I was lightheaded.

Granny hummed and hawed down the phone, side-eyeing her son. 'No, Margaret, the children are to stay here for now, Davy said.'

My mum told me later she was begging to collect us. She told me later that she had rung Davy and he had told her she would never see us again.

I don't know how long we were in Granny Tweed's for, but it felt like forever. My mum kept calling and calling and getting refused access to us, not even for a visit. What was Granny Tweed thinking? She knew what my mum was being put through, she had seen it. Yet she still did what her violent, abusive son decided on. I don't think, as a woman and as a human being, I can ever understand that.

One day my mum called and Davy's sister Diana picked up the phone. I remember her going quiet as my mum spoke to her, her fingers twisting through the phone cord, as she wrapped it around her pointing finger while she listened to my mum's pleas down the phone. Then she started whispering with her face turned away from us. The next day when we came out of school it wasn't Davy's sister there waiting, as we had been told, it was my mum.

When I say I was on cloud nine walking back to Granny Boyd's, that's an understatement. We all were.

We barely got to sit down in Granny Boyd's when Davy came through the door, face on fire, his teeth and his fists clenched.

'Get in the car children,' he said, 'right now, and you ...' he pointed at my mother.

'Davy, now ...' Granny Boyd attempted appeasement, but she may as well have been talking to the wall.

Davy got my mother by the elbow and said, 'You don't want your mother to have trouble now, do you? Not in her lovely home here.'

It was a threat.

My mother held her own for a minute, staring at the floor. Perhaps she was thinking about what he said, perhaps she was stealing herself for the beating she would get later. Then she took the little ones by the hand, said 'come on' to me, and we went outside and got into Davy's car.

Around that time Davy got his first cap for Ireland. And around that time the media, people in school, people on the street, started to talk about Davy personally and used words like 'gentleman' and 'great man' about him. Children I knew saw him as a hero. They waved at him and shouted, 'Good man Davy.' People idolised him. When my brother, Aaron, would come home, he would talk to Davy like that too, like he was a fan in the presence of his hero.

I could not stand it. How could they look at Davy and not see what I saw? The devil. He was a wolf in sheep's clothing. Sometimes I would ask myself, who was Davy, really? Was he the person I knew or the person they knew? I still don't know the answer.

My mum had another baby, my sister Victoria. As with Catherine, she had her very quickly, and afterwards she had a really hard time. She haemorrhaged again with this baby and was terribly sick. When I saw her in the hospital after, she was wrapped in a tin-foil blanket, ashen-faced and with a tube feeding donated blood into her arm.

The baby was perfect and so tiny. I was fifteen and so I brought her everywhere with me, often getting scowls and frowns from people who mistook her for a baby of my own. I didn't mind, I wanted to mind her. My friends and I would argue over pushing the pram. At that stage I was doing a childcare course in a nearby college, and I had it in my head that I wanted to do something good and become a social worker. I wanted to protect children like me.

Our family had outgrown our house and with Davy doing so well, he decided to put money into renovating and adding to it. For the time that was happening, we all moved in with Davy's sister Diana and her husband. There were four bedrooms in her house and so we had loads of space and it was nice to stay there.

Diana was what I would call a homely woman. When this all happened, she was newly married and putting in great effort as a wife. But to be honest, she was hardly much older than me and so we ate breakfast together, took the journey to college together and then all of us would have dinner together. She always helped my mum with us, acting like I would, like a big sister. My mum seemed safe there – the way it was all going smoothly lowered Davy's temper and things were, for that while, calmer for my mum. I will say I think all of us worried a little bit about going back, but we wondered would the new house, with more space, make a difference.

The changes were good ones. My brother's bedroom had been knocked through to make the kitchen bigger and there was a dining space now. The bathroom had been extended. There were two new bedrooms put into the attic for me and Lorraine. My new room was blue and green. I loved it.

In the newly refurbished bungalow, with a space of my own, it wasn't long before Davy ruined that room for me, too. He had stopped creeping in during the night, but now he would barge in at all times, hoping to catch me changing, and if he did he would stand there staring as I pulled my clothes on. He would say the word 'sorry', but he didn't mean it and he didn't move. He would just stand there with such a hard expression on his face – one of absolute power.

He made sure he kept our own people at a distance. Really close family from my mum's side eventually took a step back. Even Uncle Danny, who had lived with us, eventually unable to keep himself calm when Davy would put his little girl down, stopped calling in. Davy had called Gemma a little brat, and it just wasn't true. But Davy was enamoured with Victoria, and looking back now, knowing what I know, I suppose I could find reasons for that.

Back then I was watching my sisters like a hawk, but I just didn't see what I should have seen, even though I was looking really hard. I suppose I was a child, and so the ideas I went with came from a childish mind. I believed that because I was not Davy's daughter he abused me, and they were, so he didn't. But Lorraine was terrified of Davy. She would flinch and look for someone to stand behind when he came into the room. Catherine didn't look for him and she pulled away if he caught her for a kiss on her cheek. Yet Victoria adored her daddy, putting her arms out for him the moment he came through the door.

Davy's reputation as a family man, a good Protestant and a great hero of sport was given a further boost when he stood up for his community against the police during the protests that happened every year during the Orange marches. Now he was a man of the people. He picketed the chapel in Harryville, Ballymena, and shouted abuse at the churchgoers on their way to Mass. He shouted over and over again at the priests who said Mass there, 'Paedophile! Paedophile!'

Davy grew popular in the community and, with the encouragement of locals, he decided to run as a DUP councillor for Harryville. This meant a number of things. Firstly, he was busier than ever before and so out of the house a good bit, which meant an easier time for us.

One night the phone rang and Davy warned me, 'Do not say I am here.' He was supposed to be at work but was home.

'Hello?' I answered the phone.

A man's voice honked down the phone. 'Can I speak with David Tweed please?'

'He's not in at the minute,' I said. I looked across at Davy, doing as I was told. 'Can I take a message?' I asked the man.

'If you could ask him to call Ian Paisley back when he can.'

'Of course, Ian,' I said, knowing exactly who he was, and that Davy would want to take this call, but, feeling a small sense of power, I decided that orders were orders. 'I'll get him to call you.'

We said goodbye and the call ended, I hung up.

'You've to call Ian Paisley,' I said.

All hell broke loose, but that small moment of power was worth it.

I decided then I was going to put a lock on my door and I was going to do it myself. I told my mum a story about the little ones messing in my room and asked her to bring me to the hardware shop near us and she did, letting me test the handles and work out which one would do, and then buying it for me. The one I chose had a key for the outside, but it was a thumb-turn lock on the inside – exactly what I wanted.

I fitted that lock myself, feeling a huge surge of self-esteem when I did, even though it took me a while and it was not easy. Every time I was in my room, I would turn that lock and feel – for the first time – safe from Davy.

Davy was elected as a councillor for Harryville in 1997. He had a lot going on. He was playing for Ulster. Though his success with the Irish team was short-lived, it had an impact, with four caps and huge popularity among men in his community. He was training, attending the council meetings, going to meetings for the Orange Order, the Apprentice Boys and the Black Preceptory. The sides of Davy, the one we knew and the one they knew outside, I think those were the same side. It was just that his ferocity and need to control things worked for the community, but it worked against us. And when things wouldn't go smoothly for him outside the house, he took his frustrations out inside.

'Where is she?'

I knew that question, and it always meant my mum was about to get beaten up. She could be anywhere – in the kitchen making his tea, upstairs making the beds, in the bathroom cleaning his shit and piss off the toilet. It didn't matter if he hadn't seen her all day, or if their last words to one another were pleasant ones. If Davy had something happen outside the house, like if someone made him feel small, he would find his wife and work on his self-esteem.

This one day, he had been in the bedroom speaking with someone on the phone for a while. My mum was hanging up washing outside and I heard Davy hang up the phone with a cheery goodbye. There was less than a beat and then he bellowed, 'Where is she?' He stormed from the bedroom across the living room.

I kept my eyes on the TV, but then I heard the back door swinging. So I turned off the TV and I followed him out. *This was not fair.*

I heard a bang from the end of the garden, and my mum's familiar sob and the baby started crying.

No way. Not today.

My mum was against the wall of the house, Davy had her by the shoulders, her heels were off the ground. Victoria was screaming, standing too close with her fist clutching my mother's cardigan.

'I won't have it!' Davy said, about whatever it was that he had decided was my mum's fault.

The next thing I knew the air stopped, time stopped and I stood there without the ability to move. Davy had taken his hands off my mother's shoulders and put them around her neck, and he was choking the life from her. There, in her own back garden, with her family's washing moving in the breeze and the sun in the sky, she was going to die.

My body came back to me and I grabbed Victoria roughly and ran her into the house. I put her down in the kitchen, pointed in her face and said, 'Stay here Victoria do not come back out.' She nodded, wringing her little fat hands and wailing so hard.

As I turned to go back out to help my mum, she flew in through the open door past me and into the hall. Davy came behind her. I used the sofa to lever myself and as he passed by I jumped onto his back, spitting and screaming like a wild cat, scratching and pulling at his hair and face and neck. I was full of adrenaline and anger, and I was letting him know about it.

I may as well have been made of feathers with the ease with which he plucked me off and threw me across the room, landing me with a thud against the TV unit. It wobbled but didn't fall over. I was winded and gasping. I wanted to kill him. I could hear the sounds of my mum being beaten in the bedroom, but I couldn't move, there was no breath in my lungs and I curled into a ball to try to get it back. With a final bang and a thud, the sounds from the bedroom stopped and Davy walked back into the room I was in, the neck of his rugby jersey pulled out of shape, his face red and his lungs heaving. His mouth was open and closing like a fish on a pier, and he grabbed his keys and cards and walked out of the house. I heard the car go, it drove away. I crawled across the room and pushed myself up to standing using the sofa.

I heard my mother's sobs before I saw her. She was standing at the living-room door, her eye closed up, her lip burst. She was holding her shoulder with her opposing hand and had her head angled back to look at me from under her swollen brow.

'Did Davy hit you?' she asked, her breathing too fast. She was gulping air between words.

'Don't worry about me,' I said. My legs were shaking with the adrenaline still pumping through me. 'I'm grand, he just threw me off him.'

My mum started to shake her head and mutter. That was the step too far. Davy didn't know it, but that was the line. My mum knew that she had to go now. She knew the next time Davy put his hands on her neck would be the last breath she took.

She crossed the hall into her bedroom where the phone was and picked it up. Her finger pressed three times into the dial.

'Police please,' she said as calmly as if she were making a normal phone call, 'I need someone to come.'

10

Refuge

There was a women's refuge in Coleraine and the police sent a taxi to take my mother there with the three youngest. The police didn't even come to the house and no charges were ever made against Davy then or, as far as I know, ever.

The women's refuge had the space they said, but only for my mum with the three small ones. I was seventeen and seen as a separate case. They would bring me in as soon as they could. At first my mum shook her head and said to the care worker on the phone that she couldn't leave me in the house – she was genuinely afraid of what would happen to me if she did that.

'Mum you go, I'll lock my door,' I said.

'Sure your door won't hold him back – if he wanted to break it, he could,' she said.

'He won't,' I said, 'I'll call the police if he does anything.'

I just wanted her to go. I wanted her to get out, now.

My mum packed bags, while I minded the baby, and as soon as my sisters came through the door from school she called a taxi and they were gone.

The house felt huge and scary. I stood in the middle of it wondering and worrying about what was going to happen when

Davy got back. I rang Uncle Danny and told him.

'Sure, come stay here, Amanda,' he said.

'I can't do that to you and your family, Danny,' I said, 'God knows what he is going to do ...' I had no idea.

'Well, any trouble, come over,' he said. I said I would.

I went up the stairs and locked myself in my room.

I heard Davy's car in the distance and I braced myself. The dull clip of the door closing, the sound of his keys, the front door closing behind him. I heard movement downstairs, drawers being opened and shut.

'Margaret?' I heard him call out. 'Margaret are you home? Amanda?'

I held my breath.

He came up the stairs, paused at the top for a few beats and then I heard him charge through Lorraine's door. Another pause, then the floorboards creaked as he stepped back out of the room.

He tried the handle of my door. It was locked.

'Are you in there?' He shouted it.

I stared at the door. Would he come through it if I didn't answer? Probably.

'I am,' I said.

He changed his tone, faked a gentle voice. 'Can I come in?' he said.

'No, I'm changing in here,' I said.

'I'll wait till you're dressed and you can open it,' he said. I could hear how strained his 'gentle' tone was. I could hear that he was seething.

'What do you want?' I asked.

'Where is your mother and my girls?' he said. It was dinner

time, he knew something was up, there had not been many times when my mum wasn't in the kitchen cooking his meal to appease him, to avoid getting punched and kicked.

'I have no idea,' I said back as bravely and nonchalantly as I could muster, when the truth is I was terrified.

'Where are they, Amanda?' he said again.

'I'm telling you, I don't know,' I said and it was with confidence, because I actually didn't know. I was answering the question I wanted, not the one he was asking. My mum was in a refuge, but I spoke as though Davy was asking me whereabouts in town she was, and I had no idea.

I stayed in my room all night, hungry and worried. Davy came up a few more times to ask me where my mum and my sisters were, and I gave him the same answer. I stayed awake all night, one eye on the door, scared that it would lift off its hinges with a kick. If I had relaxed even a bit, I would have fallen asleep and I just couldn't risk it. It had been so long since I'd woken up with his shadow over me, I couldn't bear the thought of that happening again.

I decided to leave the house the next day, to see my friends and hang around in their houses, where people weren't volatile and cruel. I had a boyfriend, Gavin, but he was away, and so before I left the house I called him.

'My mum is in a refuge,' I told him. 'I can't say where, but I am going too, and I'll call you when I'm there.' I didn't give him any details I was so worried that the phones were tapped. I wouldn't have put it past Davy.

That night I came home late and went straight up to my room and locked the door before Davy had time to look up from the TV.

He didn't follow me up. I'd say he was working out his plan, I'd say he was biding his time.

On Sunday I wanted to do the same again, but Davy shouted up to me, before I was even out of bed, that I was due at the farm with him for dinner. Being a teen is a strange experience – you really have no idea that you are autonomous and so, at least for me anyway, you do what you're told even in the strangest situations. In the car he asked me again to tell him where my mum was. He looked concerned, but I couldn't trust him. I said nothing at all.

When we arrived at the farm, I realised quickly it was some sort of intervention, although I wouldn't have known that word.

'You need to tell us where your mum is,' Granny Tweed said.

'I don't know where she is,' I said, and she shook her head.

'Of course you know,' Granny Tweed said. 'The girls might be in danger there. It's the right thing to tell her husband where your mother has taken his children.'

'I haven't heard from my mum. I don't know where she is.'

I filled my plate with potatoes, cabbage and meat and started eating it. They stopped asking. After that Davy brought me back to the bungalow and I went straight upstairs to my room and locked the door. I immediately burst into tears. I missed my mum, I missed my sisters, I was scared in that house. I started packing a bag, pulling my drawers out and pouring the contents into it. Then another one. I was not staying here, I'd go to Belfast as soon as it was light.

And so I did.

Before my first class the next morning, I asked my tutor if I could speak to her alone.

'I left home,' I said. 'My mum ... I don't know where she is exactly but she had to go to a refuge ... her husband was causing trouble.' I explained as best I could, but I was also afraid of explaining too much. I was always responding to my own conditioning, do not tell or else.

The tutor was kind. 'Let me give you some money, and why don't you use the phone in the office to ring your family.'

I rang Auntie Susan.

'Your mum is all right,' she told me.

I was on the verge of tears, so it took me a minute to speak back to her. I said, 'I just need to speak to her.'

'Come up to Granny's, after college, stay there,' Susan said.

When I did, my mum rang me there.

'It's grand here, Mo,' she said, 'there'll be a room for you soon, I'm sure of it, they keep saying it.'

I remember how tight I held the phone and how light her voice sounded. My little sisters were trying to tell me things through the receiver all at once.

My mum said, 'Come to Coleraine as soon as you can on Monday, call from the phone in college at two p.m. and I'll meet you off the train.'

It was a plan.

The refuge was on the outskirts of Coleraine, still close enough to walk into the town, but there weren't any shops there, so we got taxis back and forth to fetch what we needed in the way of groceries and supplies. The interior of the building was plain and simple, with very basic decor and fittings. The room my mum was in had two sets of bunk beds in an L-shape against the walls.

There was a window directly across from the door and under that was a cot. Everything was clean and simple. There were plain bed linens, a small rug on the floor and drapes that fell exactly to the windowsill. It was nobody's room and everybody's room. There was a shared bathroom and a shared kitchen, with everything we required. There were friendly staff, all women, which was good.

It was exactly the safe, warm space that we all needed.

It felt strange to be there, and a little awkward, but I was so glad of it, so glad to be back with my mum and my sisters. In order to make sure nobody followed me back there, I stayed at the refuge all the time and didn't go to college.

Me and my mum made meals together and fed the girls things like nuggets and fish fingers with chips, or mince and onions and carrots and mash – still a favourite of mine. Food in the refuge tasted so good to me. It might have been the absence of fear that had that effect.

Sometimes a few of the women and their children would eat together, clubbing their money together for ingredients and making a big pot. We could eat what we wanted, without having to worry about what Davy might say or do if he was in a mood.

In the refuge I was classed as an adult, even though I was still a child, but it really gave me a boost to be classed that way. I took on responsibility there with pride and determination to do a great job. I hoovered and cleaned common areas, often when they didn't even need them, and I helped the other mothers with their children, and babysat while they went into town to get groceries in peace. It felt like we were all in the one boat, and I suppose we all were. That was our common ground, escaping from suffering.

It was my first experience of camaraderie. I have never forgotten how much I thrived in the company of those women.

We weren't there long, when my mum – I'd imagine from all the years of being trampled on – started to struggle emotionally.

'I just wonder are they missing their daddy?' she said to me one day as we chopped vegetables sitting at the big table in the refuge kitchen. I swear my heart stopped when she said that and the knife I was using fell out of my hand.

I looked at my sisters playing under the window near us, a Barbie in each hand, chatting away among themselves. There was something in their expression that I hadn't seen before. Looking back now I think it was that they were not on their guard, like we all had been, for Davy.

'I just worry that they'll be missing him,' my mum said. 'I might speak to Nora about it.' Nora was the counsellor in the refuge.

'Mum, he might find out where you are,' I said.

'Maybe I'll just let them call him,' she said.

But I knew. My mum was going to go back to him. I could feel it. When I first arrived at the refuge, she was lighter and brighter and almost giddy with the feeling of safety. But after a while, as the days went on, her eyes darkened and she spoke in a lower voice. I knew what she was feeling because I was feeling it too – it was anxiety. I suppose, maybe, in the complicated thing that is the human mind, we both felt anxious because we didn't know what was going to happen. At least at home we did, even though it was bad.

I know my mother felt guilt and shame too, for being a wife who ran away. Communities have never really allowed that kind of thing to prevail, and all of those thoughts that people have because of their conditioning – thoughts about women and what they are to be blamed for – my mum and I had those same thoughts about ourselves. Davy Tweed was a pillar of the community; he was a good Protestant man. We were the trouble-seeking runaway women holding his daughters hostage. My mother's guilt was over the break-up of this family. Even with the circumstances, she was seen as not working hard enough on a marriage.

In the refuge I don't think I really understood what way my mother was thinking, but I knew she was struggling. I wrote a poem while I was there, on a scrap of paper that I still have.

Through the Eyes of a Child
I hear her cries, but what am I to do
I'm helpless up here in my room
I'll just curl up on my bed and squeeze my teddy tight,
I just cover my ears, so I don't hear the fight.
But it's no use, I can still hear her cries,
So, I curl up smaller and close my eyes.
Why does he have to hurt her so much?
How could anyone deserve such a punch?
It's all my fault she's stuck in this fight,
Why can I not just do something right?
I'm too scared to go get help,
Oh God no! Not another yelp
Please just stop, don't hit her again
Are they all so deceiving, this race of men?
Stop it, stop it, I feel so bad
It's my fault, I put this beast in my stepdad.

I shouldn't have upset him before,

Then my mum wouldn't have been knocked through the
door.

Here I am up here feeling sorry for myself,

And my mum's down there with her life on the shelf.

The screaming has stopped, the door slams shut.

Mummy I'm sorry for keeping you in this rut.

Oh Mummy! Look at your face what have I done?

How could anyone do this to their mum?

Mummy I'm sorry for what has happened to you,

I hope you find it in you to forgive me,

Mummy, please, will you?

Amanda Tweed (28 March 1998)

At that point I became really angry with myself for not telling her about my abuse the second I arrived in that refuge. It was too late now, I thought, because she would think I was making it up to stop her going back. I hadn't said anything at first because when I arrived, I think I was so relieved to see everyone happy I put it off. I wanted to tell my mum; I had always wanted to tell my mum. I just had an immature mind and it wasn't able to put things into order or perspective.

Once my mum let the girls call Davy on the phone, he would spew his apologies and promises down it into my mother's ear. I'd hear him, a stream of non-stop word salad from his mouth – I really think it was a type of brainwashing. I really believe that he was almost hypnotising her when he did that, she became so placid and malleable when he spoke like that. His words would come so fast, and he would repeat sentences over and over and get her to repeat them back. It was a tactic. He told her he hadn't been eating and that it was making him ill, he was losing sleep and nothing was right in the world with her gone.

'Mum, please,' I said when I saw she was giving in, 'please let's stay here. It's better here, we can find our own house.'

'Davy said he will go to marriage counselling,' she said. 'He said he needs me.'

Eventually he convinced her to let him see the girls, and when she brought them, he arrived with flowers for her. Anytime he got to be around her, just before letting her leave, he would hold her hand and spill the same drivel he was using down the phone.

'Name your price, Margaret,' he would say to her. 'Whatever it takes, I'll do it, please just come back.'

So we did. There was no price. Not really. Once we got home, Davy's plans for counselling didn't last long, with maybe three visits, and the promise to go to anger management was broken.

'I'm a councillor here in this county,' he said to my mum when she brought it up. 'Do you want me to lose that position once I'm spotted going in and out of an anger management course?'

Back in the bungalow I stayed in my room whenever I was at home. I had nothing much going on, I had dropped out of college when we were in the refuge and had only been able to find a part-time job one day a week, so for the rest of the time I just sat up there. I was waiting. I knew the violence would come back and I wanted to be there when it did.

The clock in my room would tick loudly as the hours came and went. I didn't play music, I didn't write or read, I just sat waiting for the sound. The scuffle, the drag, the sob. I sat on my bed or on the floor and stared at my door, digging my nails into my arm until I'd draw blood. I was waiting. I'd bite into my lip – the feeling felt good to me. I thought about why I was alive. I thought about the rest of my life and I didn't want to live it. The idea of living, which for me was simply waiting to bury my mother, was impossible. I can't say I wanted to be dead, but I didn't want to live this way, and I was so young I didn't understand that I could have a good life. I believed fully that my life was this.

Then one day I noticed a knife on a plate that was by my door waiting to go down. I had accidentally brought it up with the sandwich I'd made and would pretend to have eaten.

I pressed the knife down into the flesh of my arm and dragged it sideways.

11

A Life of My Own

My mum noticed the end of the cut on my forearm when I reached over for the TV remote. Davy wasn't home, so I had come downstairs and we were in the living room watching whatever was on.

'What happened your arm?' she asked me.

'I caught it on a wire, on the way back from work,' I said. The knife had only scratched me, the blade dulled from years of use.

'Jesus ... it looks bad,' she said.

I pulled my sleeve down and caught it with my fingers into a ball and made a fist around it, 'It's not bad, doesn't hurt.'

She looked at me for longer than she normally would, longer than was comfortable.

'What?' I said.

'You seem quite low in yourself,' she said, 'and you've lost so much weight ... you're really skinny, Amanda.'

'I'm fine,' I said, 'I'm not skinny.'

'Would you pop down to see the doctor would you?' she said.

'I seen him last week,' I said.

'Did he give you something?'

'No,' I said.

'I think you should ask him for something,' she said, 'stop you feeling so low.'

'I'm not taking anything, Mum,' I said.

'If you're feeling bad ... what he gives you will make you feel better ...' she persisted.

'Do you feel better?' I asked her. 'He gave you pills, did they work?'

She looked back at the TV and turned the station over.

I stared at her. It was only a matter of time until Davy beat her again. I knew that. I knew that and now I also knew that when he did, I wouldn't be here.

'Olivia called me yesterday and asked me to come over,' I said. My aunt had recently moved to England.

My mum nodded.

'She needs help with the kids, I think I'm gonna go,' I said.

'That's a good plan then,' my mum said. 'Do you the world of good to get away.'

I left for England the following week. Just before I went, my mother told me she was expecting again. There was another child on the way. It took me a while to congratulate her because my heart was on the floor when she told me. When she said it, the key to this prison we were in turned again, locking us in for longer. Our sentence was being extended.

I mustered up a smile, told her I was delighted, and I suppose that wasn't a lie, as the babies my mother had were my beautiful siblings, whom I loved more than anything. This one would be no different. But it was harder to leave knowing that she was so vulnerable again. I decided not to stay away too long.

I spent my time in England worried. I still wasn't eating, I was still controlling food and harming my skin. Animals who are trapped and frustrated chew at their limbs and I was no different. As soon as I could, as soon as my aunt said I could go home, I went.

For the first time in my life when I got in the door from the airport my mother hugged me and then she started crying. At the time I thought it was with relief that I was back, now I think it was because I was not even six stone.

'I missed you, Mo,' she said. Victoria ran up and hugged my legs and I patted her soft curly hair and told her I had missed her.

When my mother let go of me, I noticed her bump. 'You've popped something shocking,' I said to her.

She looked at me too. 'Did Olivia not feed you? You're skinnier than you were when you left.'

'All the running around after the kids.' I fobbed her off.

My youngest sister, Jamiee-Leigh, was one of those chubby babies, the ones with plenty of fat whose folds make it look as though their hands and feet are screwed on, the ones that feel like sandbags when you lift them. She was adorable.

Not long after she was born, my mum's family were thrown into chaos. My cousin, who was nine, had been rushed into hospital when her mum found her unresponsive in her bed one morning. At six, despite appearing perfectly healthy, she had suffered her first stroke, a consequence of malformed arteries bringing blood to her brain too quickly and causing aneurysms that would strike more than once.

Of course, everyone rushed to the hospital, and so little Jamiee-Leigh was left most of the time in my care while my mum stayed with her sister down at the Royal Hospital in Belfast. It was a really tough time for that side of our family.

I remember the reverend from our church arriving at the hospital to pray over my darling wee cousin, lying there helpless with tubes and wires attached to her arms and legs and a breathing apparatus in her throat. She was so ill.

Then the same man, the following week in church, ranted from his pulpit in a long sermon about how the sins we commit anger God and that anger manifests in our early deaths ... something he said he knew from the story of nine-hundred-year-old Noah. He started preaching about how babies are born sinners, and that being a practising Christian is the only way to appease God.

I didn't know what to do with the anger that boiled up in me when I heard the minister spout that rubbish out of his flapping mouth. What kind of level of evil could he have inside of him to maintain that those who die young deserve it? My wee cousin, down in the hospital, fighting for her life, had done nothing. I knew what that minister was saying was wrong. I knew he was talking pure shit, standing up there waving his arms and indoctrinating people with bad ideas.

I clenched my fists and teeth sitting there listening to that. This same reverend had laid a hand on her in so-called prayer and now, here in church, he was accusing her of being so bad-minded that God had struck her down? Was he mad? Did he believe that? He knew that men like Davy existed and walked around free of this 'wrath of God', so he must have known this theory couldn't add up. Why was he preaching this now? Was he trying to explain away my cousin's illness away by blaming her for it? What exactly had she done?

I had had run-ins with this reverend before. His hellfire and brimstone always set my teeth on edge.

I sat there with Davy's family sitting around me, a man who rarely set foot in a church, a man who they knew battered and tortured his wife, a man I knew was bad to the core of his being, and I felt rage. No *fucking* way was I listening to this shit. I got up and walked out.

I knew immediately there was no sense in this place. I knew going to church was a meaningless and reckless activity that I would never partake in ever again. Any ideology that blames a baby for her illness is not only a bad one, it's evil.

A week later that same reverend came to our house and asked me why I had left his church in the middle of his sermon. I told him why.

'You remember Arlene Woods?' he said.

'No, I don't,' I said.

'The girl who was killed in that crash up outside Dervock,' he said. I knew who he meant then, and I nodded and said so.

'Do you want to die in a crash like that?' he said, and my mouth fell open. I had no idea what he was asking me that for.

'Going against God with a lifestyle of nightclubs and boyfriends is a sin,' he said. 'That's why she was killed – she rejected God's teachings and angered him.'

'You're crazy,' I said, 'God is love.'

He shook his head and wagged his finger, 'You'll end up burning in hell with her!' Then he looked at me as though I actually was the devil. 'Church will save you.'

I never went back to that church.

I'd been close to a boy for nearly a year before my mum went into the refuge, and the relationship continued even though he was working in England. It was a nice feeling, having a boyfriend, and despite there being so much time spent not seeing each other, neither of us wanted anything but to be together. I loved seeing him when he came back for a weekend, he loved seeing me too. I got a job then in the civil service, and it seemed I was on some sort of path to a life of my own. I wouldn't say life was good, but it was tolerable.

Since my mum came back from the refuge, Davy hadn't beaten her, but he was starting his old ways again, starting to grind her down. He would always make these so-called jokes – he did it to me about my weight and he did it to my mum about her mothering. 'Aw, bad Mummy,' he would say whenever she corrected the girls or told them off.

My mum never roared or shouted, but she could be stern for our own sake and safety. Davy always made something of that, especially when we came back after leaving him. So my mum stopped correcting and chastising, and my little sisters started walking all over her. Of course they did – kids do that when they have no boundaries set for them. Children will push until they find out where the boundary is, and in our house eventually, it was nowhere.

Davy also convinced my mum somewhere along the way that he had the power to take her kids and that nobody would support her if she left him again.

I never looked at my mum and thought anything about her mental state or what she was thinking. Her life with Davy was my whole life. There wasn't another mother that I knew, just this sad and worn down one. I never expected better of her, I never wanted to shake her or tell her to buck up. How she was, was how she was. It was our norm. At no point in my childhood did I feel let down by my mum. I think I saw that there was danger and I knew she needed protecting, but it wasn't in her control as far as I saw it. It was only as I got older that I thought more about it in that way.

Davy wasn't playing much rugby anymore and he wasn't hitting my mum anymore. Maybe he was protecting his reputation, maybe she was just as low as he wanted her to be and there was no need. She was a broken pony, a worn-down animal. She did what she was told, when she was told.

He kept her, and us, down with threats and verbal abuse. We knew not to cross him.

He was cruel.

At times my mum would leave us all down to Granny's, or to Aunt Susan's, and she could be gone for the whole day and never say why. That was strange, especially when I was old enough to mind everyone on my own. So I used to worry when she was gone, knowing something was wrong. She told me years later she was trying to pluck up the courage to kill herself during those times. She never quite found it, thank God.

12

Happiness Shattered

When I was twenty I was convinced I would be with my boyfriend Gavin forever. He was back after a year in England and we were full on.

'Will we get a dog?' I suggested, too young to get married, not earning enough to move in together, and wanting something to bind us together.

We wanted a Rhodesian Ridgeback. I had seen one around and thought it was beautiful, and you know how it is in your early twenties, you thrive on spontaneity. But, of course, my boyfriend still lived in his parents' house and I still lived in mine, and neither of us had the money to get our own flat, even though we dreamed about it. He couldn't keep a dog in his house, as his sister was really scared of them, so I asked at home and to my surprise Davy was all into it.

'Aye, no problem,' he said.

'Are you sure? The dog would have to live in the house,' I said.

'No problem at all.' He really seemed to agree. 'It can sleep in the conservatory.'

So I got my puppy – big, lumbering, all legs and ears, huge paws that tripped him up and antics that would have you in stitches. I called him Buster.

Buster loved everyone, and as he met people his tail would whip your legs so hard it would hurt. He loved children, the elderly, everyone on the street knew his name and he had a lick for everyone. Except Davy.

It's funny how dogs can sense a bad person. Maybe it's body language or just some innate ability to know what danger smells like, but Buster couldn't tolerate Davy. When Davy came into a room, Buster would slink out of it, his tail between his legs, his ears flattened back. If I was on the couch, Buster would stand between us.

'Come here, Buster,' Davy would shout, but my dog would just stand there, eyes locked on Davy.

'That dog is not right,' Davy would tell me and everyone else. I think the dog made Davy uncomfortable; honestly, I do. I think the way the dog acted made him feel really unnerved. He thrived on control and bullying, and you can't work that with a dog who doesn't see you as his master. Buster knew who the boss was in his world, and that was me. Davy was nothing more than someone to be avoided.

So Davy told me to get rid of him. He said it as though Buster was a full bin or an old coat. 'That dog will have to go.'

I ran out of the house in floods of tears, Buster whining on the end of his leash. I walked so fast, I was so upset and so pissed off. Would I ever be free of this shit?

With lungs full of sobs, I found myself at my boyfriend's house, and his mum, Joan, answered the door.

'Gosh, are you alright love?' she said and brought me in. Buster was delighted, his whole body wagged once he realised he was in his favourite place.

'I can't keep Buster, Davy won't have him in the house any-more, he said so,' I wailed.

Joan made me tea, patted my shoulder and listened to my woes. I cried my eyes out sitting there, Gavin pacing the floor with frustration. He knew I loved my dog and he loved me. I could see he had no answers, not just yet anyway.

I slept with Buster in the bed with me that night, heartbroken. He looked so vulnerable to me now, he didn't have a clue what was happening. I thought of giving him away to strangers and I sobbed. There was no way I could do that. I'd rather sleep under a bridge than give my puppy away. But even though I was determined to figure it out, it felt like I had no way to.

As soon as I was up, I rang my only support – Gavin.

'Bring him up for a bit,' he said, 'and try not to worry.'

By the time I got up there, he had good news.

'I spoke to them,' he said and nodded toward his dad, who was cutting the grass with an enthusiastic Rhodesian Ridgeback following him up and down the garden.

I nodded.

'Buster can stay here for now,' he said, 'but he will have to have a kennel, and we have to clean up after him and if he breaks anything, replace it.'

I exhaled, not realising I had been holding my breath the whole time he had been talking to me. Then it was all go. We bought him a kennel and bits and bobs for it, and then we went down to my house to get his things. The problem was solved.

A few days later Davy said, with a grin, 'You'd miss Buster around the place, wouldn't you?' He really was just a horrible, cruel man.

Not long after that it was Christmas. I was spending more and more time up at my boyfriend's, even when my boyfriend wasn't there, to see Buster as well as him. His family were so good to me and on Christmas morning they had presents for me too, and they waited to exchange them until I called in. We were all sitting around and Gavin handed me a shoebox, wrapped up with a bow. His family all went quiet and all eyes were on me as I unwrapped it, so I knew something was up. I thought it was going to be some sort of prank, I was waiting for the spring to pop and the box to explode or something. But I just unwrapped one layer after another until I was left with a small card with a message saying, 'To my fiancée at Christmas', which I didn't really notice as I opened it, aware that suddenly everyone was staring at me. Inside was a ring hanging on a piece of ribbon and the words, *Will you marry me?*

I was so happy. We had some champagne and then we went over to show my mum the ring, with its sparkling diamond. A sparkle that dulled as soon as Davy appeared.

'You only got that because I said I approved it,' he said, and I realised Gavin had asked Davy for permission. My stomach felt hot and I had to sit down. I wanted to give the ring back – it was tainted.

When we brought the dog for a walk, I asked him, 'Why did you do that? Why ask him?'

'Well, that's what you're supposed to do isn't it?' my fiancé said. He had been simply checking boxes it seemed.

I could not simmer down, feelings boiled over.

'I'm not Davy's to give away,' I said, but I said it quietly.

Planning things with my boyfriend felt real for the first time. Would we go to Australia, would we live in Ballymoney, would we travel, or buy a house together? We decided on a house and I slept through the night for the first time in my whole life. I had a front door of my own, and only people I invited through it were welcome there. I wasn't under threat of having it kicked in. It was mine. My mum hadn't been beaten in so long there was a part of me that kind of believed those days might be over. The knot I had got so used to having in my stomach all my life was loosening and fading.

Little did I know the days to come would bring all kinds of horror.

'Hello?'

'Amanda is that you? It's me, Caroline.'

Caroline was a close friend of my mum's. One of those people who has been around your whole life and feels like family. Her daughter Emma was always in our house. We all played together so much during my childhood.

I noted a shake in her voice. I asked if things were okay.

'Not really, Amanda, I need to ask you something about your mum,' she said.

'Okay, go on ahead,' I said.

'Well, you see, it's just that ...' she paused for a minute. 'Emma has told me that your mother's husband ...' I was grateful for the distinction, 'well, you see, she said he abused her ...'

We held a silence between us for an unpleasant moment.

'And I believe her,' she said.

So did I.

'I know your mum is away right now,' Caroline said. She was right, my mother was on her first holiday, in Spain, with

Davy. Immediately I wanted everything to stop. I wanted this conversation to happen later, when Mum was back. It felt so dangerous. It felt like the pin on a grenade was being pulled out and I needed Caroline to hold fast.

'Caroline, please can you wait till she gets back?' I said. 'You know she is with Davy over there ... you know what he is like ...'

'Aye I do,' she said, 'it's why I was ringing you to ask you what you thought about it, should I tell her at all?'

'You should tell her,' I said, 'she needs to know, and she will want to know this.'

Caroline sniffed down the phone.

'Is Emma okay?' I asked her.

'She is in a state,' Caroline said in a quiet, breaking voice.

'Are you going to the police?' I hoped so, but not yet.

'No, I'll wait to talk to your mummy,' she said.

That was a relief.

'I can't believe it,' she said. 'I can't believe that ... what he did to my daughter ...'

I pressed my lips together. I didn't have any words for how I was feeling at that moment.

'Do you want me to tell her?' I said, knowing I was going on holiday to where my mum and Davy were the next week.

'I'll do it,' Caroline said. 'I want to tell her myself, in one go.'

'Okay,' I understood.

'Will he hurt her, do you think?' she said.

'Probably,' I was honest, 'but I think you should get the police as well.'

I rang my fiancé. I told him straight. I was worried about going on the holiday now, knowing what I knew was coming. How could

I sit there and talk to my mum when I knew that she was going to learn the secrets her family harboured? I knew the entire story would come out now, because I knew she would ask me. And I was not going to lie.

'Look you don't know it's true,' my fiancé said. 'Emma might be making it up.'

He was trying to comfort me. But he didn't know what I knew. And I wondered would he think that of me?

By the time we landed in Fuerteventura the knot in my stomach was tight again. The wheels touched down early in the day, and my heart started racing. My fiancé could see how tense I was.

'I thought you liked flying,' he said.

'It's not that,' I said.

'Just don't think about it, let your mum handle it.'

He had no idea.

We checked in to the hotel, and while we were standing there waiting for our keys I looked around. Out by the pool bar there were people sitting around and I scanned that crowd for my mum and Davy. But there was no sign. We went up to the room, unpacked, got changed and then we went back down. Immediately a child rushed at me, grabbing my legs. It was Victoria.

'Come over, we are over here,' she said, dragging me by the hand in the way excited children do, leaning into their stride with their heads down.

I saw my mum and I saw Davy and you would think I was about to face a firing squad the way my pulse bounded – it felt like my heart was thumping in my skull. My skin went cold, even with the hot sun on it.

I don't think anybody noticed anything different about my attitude, but I didn't say much. My fiancé was acting as though everything was fine and I wondered briefly if he believed what he said about Emma making it up. He was joshing back and forth with Davy about the resort. Davy had found a Chinese restaurant and thought we should all go.

'We have been there a couple of times already,' he said, 'it's a good spot.'

He ordered shots when we arrived and I realised after I drank mine that there were pornographic pictures on the bottom of the glass, something Davy thought was great. I think that's why he really liked the restaurant – it had nothing to do with the food, which was just alright.

The next afternoon we stayed around the pool, relaxing and reading and swimming. I found it hard to relax, but I tried my best to stop thinking about what Caroline had told me. My mum was sitting in a chair by the pool sunning herself. When we left to go up and change for dinner, she said, 'I'll stay here a bit.'

As we closed in on our apartment, we heard bangs and shouts coming from up the way.

'I think someone is in a fight,' said my fiancé.

I knew who one of the fighters was, I just didn't know who the other one was until I saw my sister Catherine landing in a heap by the door of her room, where she had been thrown by her father. She got up, red, flustered and crying, and started to run when she saw me.

'Amanda, help,' she said.

I grabbed her and put her behind me as Davy came around the door. He stopped dead when he saw me.

'You're a fucking little bitch!' he said to her, wagging his finger our way. 'See there's more of that coming!'

'He hit me,' she sobbed, 'Daddy really hit me so hard.'

I knew it wasn't just a swipe, I knew he had given her a beating. I could see red stains creeping across her jaw that would turn to bruises. She was holding her arm and was limping as we crossed into my room.

My mum appeared at the apartment door.

'What's going on?' she said.

'Ask him,' I said and my mum went across the hall to where her bedroom door was open, revealing Davy sitting crying on the bed. I gave him a filthy look and closed my door.

I said I wasn't going to dinner with my mum and Davy then. I said I was staying with Catherine in the room.

'I don't think we should get involved, love,' my fiancé said. I immediately shook his arm off my shoulder.

'If you think I'm going to be playing happy families with this shit going on, you must be mad,' I said.

I brought my sister to the restaurant in the hotel once we were sure my mum and Davy had gone elsewhere. She sat over a bowl of chips, taking ages to eat them, still reeling from the battering she had got. She flinched as the nerves settled down in her face and chewed slowly, afraid to agitate the pain. She slept in my room that night, on the sofa bed by the balcony.

I had never seen Davy turn on one of his own daughters like that, and I wasn't sure what had changed. Maybe it was her age, maybe it was something she said, but he beat on Catherine like he would on my mother. He never did that to me, and it worried me, since I knew about the revelations that were coming my mother's way. Would this be it? Would this be the moment that Davy snapped and killed every single one of us?

I had another worry. I knew how hard people could be on women and I thought about the potential for victim blaming in our own community and how that would play out for my mum and us. Would we be blamed for keeping Davy's secrets? Would we be blamed for staying silent and allowing Davy to abuse other people? I didn't sleep well for the rest of the holiday.

I knew what was coming would be the hardest road any of us had yet to take.

13

Secrets Exposed

Caroline came to see my mum.

Over the years I had sometimes wondered if my mum had suspicions about what Davy was doing in our home. Sometimes it would cross my mind and I would spend a while thinking, *does she know?*, only to conclude that she couldn't.

When Caroline told my mum her story, the reaction she got from my mum confirmed what I had hoped all along – that she never knew.

'Go straight down now to the police,' my mum said. 'Go now.'

'Do you think he did it, Margaret?' Caroline said.

'Children don't come up with things like this themselves, Caroline,' my mum said. 'The police will figure it out. Go straight there now and I'll wait to hear from you then.'

The next morning, when Davy had left and when all the girls were away to school, my mum rang the police herself and told them. She gave them Caroline's number, hung up the phone and cried her eyes out.

'You kept this from me? Why?' she asked me. I knew Caroline had mentioned our chat.

'What was I going to say, Mum?' I asked her. 'Hi, Mum, having a nice holiday? Oh, by the way, your husband fiddles with kids.'

She nodded. She understood.

'Do you believe it?' she said. 'Amanda, what do you think? Do you believe it?'

'The police will get to the truth I suppose,' I replied.

'I know, but do you believe it?' she asked again.

I shrugged. Even though this was the perfect time to tell her everything, to get all the stones and kill all the birds, I didn't. I just shook my head and sympathised and wondered if I would ever tell her at all.

'Emma isn't a storyteller,' my mum said, almost to herself, 'she is such a good child, she just isn't the type to tell a lie like that ...'

I could see the torment close in on my mother.

'How could I not see that?' she said. 'How did I not see that in him? I keep replaying things in my head to try to see ... I just ... how did I not see?'

I didn't know what scenes were playing in her head, but I knew what scenes were playing in mine. I was intensely triggered by all of this and I was struggling with guilt. If I had done what Emma had done, if I had told my mummy too, then Emma and God knows who else would not have been hurt in this way. I felt so deeply sorry for what I knew Emma had suffered, because I had suffered that way too.

A few days later a social worker arrived at our house, sent there by the police, who had launched an investigation. She had called my mum and made the appointment, and everything seemed so tense and serious in our house as we waited for her to come. Davy was out – my mum had checked his schedule for work and we knew the coast was clear. The social worker gave my mum two options to choose from but zero support for the consequences of either: Davy could leave or they would take her children away.

'He is a bit violent,' my mum said, 'I'd be worried how he would take that.'

She was looking for support from someone in a position of power, but we were all disappointed at how little was offered.

'You can decide what you want to do Mrs Tweed,' the social worker said, 'but if Mr Tweed remains in the house, we will take these children out of harm's way.'

I think back at that and I get so upset. There was a real disconnect between social services and abused people, if they thought that it was okay to force one of the abused to deal with the eviction of their abuser themselves. My mum was also a victim of this violent, abusive man – I still don't think I know the half of her story if I'm honest – and even though the services were acknowledging him as a danger, they were not offering refuge or information or even a number to call if he turned violent. They were more than happy to let my mum talk to Davy about the accusations and for her to tell him to leave. That was wrong.

My mum and I came up with a plan. She was going to confront Davy after dinner, and I would take the girls out with me to give her the space to do it. She was worried it would kick off, and I suspect she was worried he would kill her in his rage. She didn't want any of her daughters to be in danger.

'No matter who shows up, Amanda,' she said, 'keep the girls with you, alright?'

I knew she meant that one of the Tweeds might show up – that was how it had played out the last time after all. We knew exactly what side Davy's family were on, no matter what. His.

I went over that night again and took the girls home with me. I was to feed them and keep them there until I heard from my mum. They saw it as a day out, a day of fun. When they arrived, my dog went crazy with excitement, wagging his tail and bouncing around. Then we went and got movies and food and we made hot chocolate.

My fiancé was happy to have my sisters at ours. He took it as an excuse to watch funny movies and to buy ice cream and sweets. He'd known my sisters, the younger ones, since they were small. They all loved him and were always so thrilled to see Buster.

As it grew late, and I hadn't heard from my mum, despite the gnaw of concern that was growing in my belly, I put them to bed in my house. Once they were asleep, I rang my mum. I was relieved when I heard her voice.

'Well?' I said.

'He just left now,' she replied and told me that he came in from work, she had his dinner for him and sat watching him eat it before she broke the news.

'I was trying to figure out how to bring it up,' she told me, 'and eventually I just said the police had contacted me with these allegations and social services said he had to move out for now.'

'Was he shocked?' I asked.

'I pretended I didn't believe it all,' she said, 'but to be honest with you, Amanda, no the man did not seem shocked or upset hearing that at all. He just packed a bag and went.'

I was glad of that. All day I had had images of my mother

being choked again and with nobody around I worried it would go too far.

A few days later another woman, on hearing the allegations, found the courage to go to the police too. Davy had abused her as a child, she said. I felt such a conflict within myself – how did I not know this was going on? Why did I think I was the only one, and why was I still terrified to speak up? Davy's years of threats echoed in my head.

I will kill your mother.

I will burn this house with you all in it.

Would he?

As each day went on, I noticed the stress eating into my mum. She was jumpy, always watching the door, and she wasn't able to focus on what you were saying, you could almost see the thoughts racing behind her eyes.

Midway through conversations about other things she would switch the subject back to Davy.

'Do you think they'll think we had anything to do with it?' she would suddenly say to me in the middle of a chat about something different.

I shook my head and took her hand. 'Mummy, don't think that, of course not, we told the police the instant we knew, that's all we could have done.'

'That poor wee girl, living with that,' my mum said. 'I feel so guilty that it happened in our house ...'

'The only person who should feel guilty is David Tweed,' I said matter-of-factly.

But I didn't believe much of that myself. I was feeling dreadful too, deep down. I was feeling the weight of the information I had around my shoulders like a yoke. The regret of not sharing it then, the fear of sharing it now.

Mum just struggled massively with being able to accept that she hadn't known what was going on over the years in her home. It was as though her mind went into overdrive.

And then she imploded.

It's hard to describe what a breakdown looks like, because my mum didn't look like anything was wrong – she was just so quiet. She couldn't engage in conversation at all, she zoned out and stared off to the side. It was hard to see her so frustrated and upset. But we all knew that inside her head there was a wildfire. If Davy had done this to these girls in our home, had he done this to us? I think my mum knew the answer, even though when she asked we denied it. The upset inside of her grew and grew until she actually could not take her own thoughts. She collapsed.

We raced her to the hospital and she was admitted. It was up to me and Lorraine, who was nearing twenty now, along with Uncle Danny, to take over the care of the little ones – Catherine, Victoria and Jamiee-Leigh. I did the morning runs and picked up the groceries. Lorraine, who was still living at home, did the after-school care and the dinners, and Danny would drop off and pick up everyone from school. He often took Catherine with him back to his house. His girl was the same age and they played together really well. They were so close. Although, I wasn't crazy about any of the children being anywhere but home, as at that time I worried a bit that Davy would take them and run. That had been his threat for years.

My mum felt the pressure of that threat too from her hospital bed. 'Just be sure not to let them out on the road to play,' she whispered, when I told her the routine they had with the three of us. 'Davy might come.'

Visiting her in the hospital was so hard because she was so quiet. It was almost as though she was an abandoned person; there was nothing behind her eyes for so long. And then, when she started calming, when she started coming back to us, we had to lie to her face.

'Did he do anything to you Amanda?' She started asking me this same question, over and over, when she was cleaning the sink, making the tea, driving – all times when she wasn't looking at me. I would hear a halt of her breath – steeling herself – and she would ask me. She was definitely not taking me at my word, because she kept asking, at least once a day.

But to be honest all of us were feeling that the truth could send her over the edge completely in the scheme of what was happening with her mental health.

A small while after my mum came out of hospital, my brother, Aaron, came home for a bit, to see her and all of us and to get his head around the allegations that had been made against Davy.

'And I take it you believe it?' he said.

'I do, Aaron, I do,' Mum said. 'Why would any child, let alone Emma, say that out of the blue? For what? It makes no sense unless it's true …'

'It doesn't, it definitely doesn't.' Aaron was thinking, I could see that. His brow was furrowed and he was picking at the tablecloth, lifting threads with his fingernails and pulling them. Then he lifted his head and looked at me with quizzical eyes.

I said I had to go bring the dog home.

When my phone rang a while later and I saw Aaron's name come up, I knew what was coming. He came over to my house and sat at my kitchen table while I fussed with filling the kettle and getting the cups down. I spent too long at it, but he waited. I think we both knew that what was coming was not going to be easy.

'So,' he said, 'what are you thinking about all of this?'

'How do you mean?' I said, deliberately obtuse.

'Do you think it's true then?' he said.

'I don't see why anyone would tell a lie like that.'

'I suppose not,' he said. 'People would either tell on someone, or I suppose they would keep it secret.'

I knew he knew. I could tell by the way he was phrasing things. The question he wanted to ask hung in the air between us. I kept my back to the room, stirring coffee that didn't need stirring.

'I suppose people do,' I said, trying to sound distant from the subject but not achieving that. I set the coffee down on the table.

'Do you want a biscuit?'

'Did Davy abuse you, Amanda?' he asked.

He was looking me straight in the face and I was looking back at him. The room, the world outside, the entire universe went totally still for the moment it took for my eyes to give me away.

Then everything swung back into action with a bang and the world became really loud, my heart clamouring in my chest and bounding in my head. It felt like I was on a rollercoaster with the way my stomach plummeted. I felt sick. I thought I would throw up if Aaron didn't look away from me, but he didn't. Not yet.

Tears formed behind my eyes and escaped, hot, onto my cheeks.

I heard my brother inhale, and then he cursed under his breath, trying and failing to keep his composure. He stood up from the table, sending it sliding forward.

'Did he? Did he abuse you?' He wasn't waiting for an answer now, he had it in the tears that fell into my tea, but I nodded anyway.

'That fucking brute, that despicable man,' Aaron said with such deep-felt emotion it changed the tone of his voice. 'What about the rest?'

I knew he meant my sisters and I shook my head. 'I don't think so.'

He pulled on his coat, cursing and shaking his head over and over.

As he left, I said, 'It'll kill Mum, don't tell her.' But he wasn't listening to me as he went out the door.

14

Pandora's Box Opens

When I realised the next day that my brother had left my house and gone to the police, I could not catch my breath. To describe how I felt is impossible. Perhaps it was a realisation that Pandora's box was open, and all the evils of the world were swirling around me. I had compartmentalised everything that had ever happened – the abuse, the times I saw my mum beaten, the crash, the fears, all of it was stored away. When I realised that Aaron had brought all of that to the police, my boxes fell and cracked open, and the entire contents of my mind spilled everywhere. I couldn't see, I could barely hear with the ringing in my ears. I couldn't speak.

I wasn't ready.

I had no idea how to pick up the pieces. All my hard work to keep myself going was shattered now. As I stood there, physically reeling, I didn't know who I was anymore. I had spent so long crafting the art of being Amanda, who had it together. Who would I be now that it was all falling apart?

The ropes of my inner self coiled against one another and knotted, deep in the pit of my gut, like they had been for most of my life.

I sat on the edge of my chair in work, for hours, staring into space, unable to concentrate, waiting for a call to come. I couldn't speak normally to anyone, I stumbled over my words and said things that made no sense because I didn't know who knew what, but I also realised I couldn't do this on my own. I thought about my sisters – what were their secrets? We had lived in the shadows for so long, all of us. I hoped I was the only victim of sexual abuse, but I knew that, regardless, we were all victims of a violent monster. Would we be for evermore known as 'those girls', the ones who were abused, the ones whose mother married the devil? I didn't want to be that, I was me, Amanda Brown – I wanted to remain myself.

My manager chatted to me about rugby, bringing Davy up with me for the twentieth time. He had no idea and was complimenting Davy, saying how great a player he was. I wondered what he would think tomorrow when this news broke, if it broke. Would he think I must be lying? Would he reject me as a human and see me as a liar? I knew secrets about his hero and they were true. My truth had to be protected too, I decided.

When the police did finally call, I went into the stairwell to take the call. I checked up above and down below and spoke quietly. The policewoman on the other end said that Aaron had made some allegations and named me as a victim of our stepfather. She was working on the case that involved Emma and the other woman, and asked would I give a formal statement?

'I don't know,' I said.

'It would be a great help to our investigation if we had all of the information,' she said.

'Can I call you back?' I said. 'I'm in work, I can't think straight ...'

113

'Take your time,' she said. 'You might want to talk to your family first, but do consider coming in. As I said, it would help.'

I hadn't been able to help these two women before and I wanted to help them now, but I was facing a storm myself, so I was unsure what path to take.

My mum called and I knew Aaron hadn't said anything to her. She was still talking about those other poor girls, and about the fact that she had heard there was a third girl who had come forward.

'Do you know who?' I asked, immediately wondering if it was me.

'Don't know, but the police said it there to Caroline,' she said. 'They told her that this girl was protecting Davy and wasn't going to make a statement.'

My blood boiled when I heard that. I wasn't protecting Davy – not even one second of my thought process went anywhere near that animal. I was trying to protect myself. If you have ever had such a secret, you might understand me. When you have spent years covering something up, it's not as easy as you think to lift the lid on it. Those lids, they are heavy.

I hoped Davy would go straight to hell.

'Caroline said the police said the third person is a daughter of Davy's,' my mother said. I could imagine her standing in her kitchen with her hand gripping the back of the chair. 'Amanda, I need the truth. I do ... I need it ... tell me now ... did Davy lay a finger on you?'

I could not form words. I couldn't breathe. The intensity of the moment overwhelmed me. My mother exhaled and I heard a wince in the sound. I didn't need to say anything – she knew. She finally knew.

'I'll come over now,' she said and hung up.

That was how my mother did 'mothering', and it is still how she does it. Being present is her love language as they say. Sure, she wasn't a tactile woman, her own sense of defence kept her from holding us for long even as children. With so many of us, I have no doubt she was exhausted by constant touch, let alone being hurt and sore most of the time from the beatings. But when you needed her, when you need her, my mother is right there.

I cleared up a bit, took the washing off the seat where I would let her sit down. I filled and boiled the kettle. Then I boiled it again. I talked to myself, rationalised the secret keeping, practised explaining why I had never told her before now. I had never doubted Davy, not once. I really had believed he was capable of murder. I believed it when he said he knew people who would cut us up. I believed that he would stop my mum keeping us if she left, and that she would have to live on the street and beg.

'But Amanda we had my parents to go to,' my mum said as we talked.

I shook my head. She hadn't lived with the parents I had. My mum, despite what she thought now, had returned to Davy over and over, and she did so to keep him from hurting her parents or destroying their home. As a child I was thinking that that was the reality, that I needed to protect everybody from him too.

Sure, intellectually I knew now that it would have probably worked out, but back then, as a wee child, there was just no way for me to look at what was happening and think the solution was anything but doing what we were told by Davy.

'I wish I could go back,' I said. 'I'd give anything to not have gone through what I did.'

'You need to go to the police, Amanda,' my mum said, and she took a long drink of her tea. We were on our third cup. The afternoon was golden outside the window, and we were two women, holding hands across a table, watching our lives fall apart.

We wanted to do the right thing. But I hadn't told my fiancé. He didn't know. How would I? What words could I use?

I stood at the door with my mum, a scared and frustrated woman feeling levels of anger she never had before in her life, knowing all the years of suffering that Davy Tweed had caused and feeling responsible.

'I am so sorry I brought him around you,' she said. 'I should have known; I should have protected you.'

'You were being abused too,' I said. 'You did all you could to get through.'

I knew as she left that she was going to confront Davy. I just hoped she wouldn't do it at home, where he would have the freedom to beat her.

A few nights later, the sound of a text message landing on my phone buzzed at the bottom of my handbag. When I pulled my phone out, I saw the message flashed up on the home screen: HE IS ON HIS WAY TO YOURS, MUM

I considered leaving him to ring the doorbell all night. I wanted to hide upstairs and not open the door at all. But when it came to it, I went down.

First, my fiancé's mother was in my kitchen, with wedding magazines, completely oblivious to the drama unfolding for me and my family.

Second, if I did ignore it and made some excuse to Joan, I was worried he would go the few doors up to where her house was and knock there. I wouldn't put it past him, so I opened the door as soon as I heard the bell.

'Can we talk?' he said. He looked smaller, and his face was red and patchy.

'About what?' I leaned on the doorframe as nonchalantly as I could. I wanted to keep things calm.

'Those girls,' he said. 'Speak to them, will you? See if they'll take it back.'

'You mean you want them to retract their statements?' I said.

'Aye,' he said, 'speak to them for me, get them to retract.'

I stood up straight. 'Sure why on earth would I do that?' I can admit now that my legs felt like jelly and my pulse was thudding in my neck so loudly I could hear it.

'I never touched any girls,' Davy said, standing there with his hands together like a little beggar boy.

Fuck you Davy. Fuck You.

I kept my cool.

'Why would I believe you over them?' I said, and I enjoyed speaking to him like that, 'Their stories match my own story, don't they? Seems true to me ...'

His eyes widened. It was almost as though he had forgotten – could that be right? His face blanched just a touch. There were beads of sweat on his forehead. He dabbed at them with the end of his tie. He never wore a tie unless he was on council business. He must have come from there.

'Have you been down to the police?' he asked, but he didn't look at me.

'That's none of your business,' I said. I knew I would go soon. He coughed.

'You'll find out if I've gone to the police soon enough Davy,' I said.

He muttered something, then got braver. 'If you've spoken to the police, that's the end of you,' he said. The usual line, the one he used with my mum and the one he had used on me.

'Is it now?' I said. 'Is that a threat?'

I noticed my hands were shaking so I shoved them into the pockets of the trousers I had on.

Davy stood there, looking small, pursing his mouth as he contemplated this sudden bravery in the daughter he was always able to coerce.

I stared him down. In the corner of my eye, I saw my mum's car pull up. She must have driven over as soon as she knew he was coming to my door. She got out of her car and walked over. Her shoulders were back and her gaze was fixed on Davy.

'Why?' she said, and I could tell she was forcing herself to stand up to him. Perhaps in a way she felt like now she was standing up for the child she thought she had let down.

'I don't know what you're talking about,' he said, stepping back from her.

'You do so,' my mum said and she raised her pointing finger towards me.

Davy shook his head hard and started to walk away down the drive, saying loudly, 'I've done nothing, I done nothing of this, nothing of this sort.'

He opened his car door and turned around.

'Are you going to believe her over me?' he said to his wife.

'Absolutely I will!' My mum shouted it.

Davy got into his car, muttering and looking over his shoulder to see who was around. Then he drove away.

'I had to come over, Amanda,' my mum said. I told her my fiancé's mum was inside and she said she didn't want to see anyone. I understood and waved her off, knowing full well from the way she was breathing that she would cry all the way home.

Before I went back inside, I took a minute. My head was floating and so I sat down on the stairs and took slow breaths. I could hear Buster scratching at the living-room door – he could clearly hear me and knew that I was distressed. Dogs are amazing that way. I let him out and focused on him, calling him a good boy and perking myself up by petting him before I went back into the kitchen.

My fiancé knew some of this, but not all at this stage, and his parents knew nothing. When I went into the kitchen, Joan said to me that I should tell my parents not to drag me into their marital troubles. I was glad she said that, as it was so far from the actual issue. She suddenly seemed so innocent sitting there thinking there was nothing more than a marital row on the cards. But I was also sad to know it wouldn't stay that way. The truth would out.

15

The Burden of Guilt

I told the police some things, but didn't make an official complaint. I told my fiancé some. I told Buster everything. I took him out for walks and I told him every single thing I could remember about my life since my mum got together with Davy Tweed. I told him how he would come into my room, I told him how he did what he did, I told him about the threats and the fear. Talking to my dog helped me sort out what had happened to me. There is something so messy about memories that have never been spoken of. They become like tangled wool, impossible to find the start or end, and with parts that are so heavy they are impossible to hold for long enough to make them out.

And in the midst of all of this turmoil, my in-laws and my fiancé were planning a wedding. It sounds absurd, but it was like there were two channels running alongside each other at that time. This deep, dark channel where everything was spilling out and dragging us down, and the other one where life was normal and carrying on as usual. The wedding was something that should have taken my mind off things, because I was so busy, and I threw myself into the preparations, focused on the wedding with my whole heart, but doing that only added to my sense of instability and, after avoiding them for years I went to the GP and got a prescription for anti-depressants.

I left my job. Davy's brother worked there, in another department, and also there was a lot of sports worship in that office. So many people had approached me prior to this all coming out to tell me they thought my 'dad' was a great guy. Now what would they say and think? I imagined conversations about me, behind my back, and I hated the thought of people going quiet when I came into the room. I just didn't want to be there. I presumed I would be excluded, and I presumed I was damned if I did and damned if I didn't. My sleep was disturbed – I would find it hard to still my mind enough to drop off, and then when I did, I would wake constantly. On Sundays I didn't sleep at all because I was so worried about what would be said in my job.

So, I got a different job, in the bank in Ballymoney. Lorraine was pregnant and I was glad to have more time to spend near her, now that I wasn't commuting so much. Her pregnancy was one bit of good news. But less than six months later my mother's mum died. Granny Boyd was gone and, really, it hit us all so hard. Her warm home where we all spent time growing up was now so quiet – no sewing machine running at the top of the stairs, no TV on. My poor mum could barely grieve with everything else that was going on. I felt so sorry for her over it all.

What made it worse was that Davy was just walking about like he had no problems at all, while we were falling apart. He was still going to his pub, still going to his council meetings; he was brazen about it. I suppose he was claiming that he was innocent and, in the way of the patriarchy, other men believed that. Davy was in the headlines because he went against his party when they signed an agreement to power share with Sinn Féin. He formed a new group with other dissenters, called the Ulster Unionist Coalition Party. He clearly wanted the status of being a party leader. It was a further step up the ladder, but, in my view, it would make for a harder fall.

My wedding came around and we flew out to Jamaica with our families to have the wedding there. It was lovely, a tonic for all of us. It felt like we had stepped out of our lives for a few weeks, and we didn't have to think about what was going on at home. We planned to have a party when we got home, and we invited everyone to it, even the relatives we had on Davy's side.

Of course, Davy was not invited. At the party, more than one of his relatives remarked how sad it was that Davy wasn't there. They knew why he was not there. I will never understand that.

The wedding really did me the world of good, I stopped taking the anti-depressants, having been nourished by the Jamaican sun and having stepped out of my life long enough to get a clear perspective. I stopped thinking about the police, I stopped thinking about the secret, I was in the honeymoon phase and focused on that.

That's when the deep, dark channel spilled over again.

I now had a husband and I still hadn't told him what my secrets were. I was, I think, worried that he would cast me off. I was worried he would be ashamed, or worse, that he would think I was telling a lie. I couldn't talk about things with my mum, as she was already struggling with guilt and regret. It was driving her demented, and I didn't want to risk pushing her into another breakdown. So, apart from my dog Buster, nobody knew the details but me. And now that my memories were unravelling and coming to the surface, they were starting to weigh me down.

I hated not being able to fully remember details, and I found it really difficult to make peace with the fact that my brain had stopped recording during the worst times and the memories were simply not there at all. Some of the memories felt like dreams, and I asked myself, were they? Were they dreams? I hoped so.

I wanted Davy in jail. That was something I was also ruminating on, spending so much time thinking about how a court case would play out, and thinking about the verdict. If he was found guilty and sent to jail, I could put everything behind me.

The court case started and my mum attended every day. In the evening I would ring her for an update and she would talk me through the evidence – how the woman and child involved had dates and times, and how Davy had provided counter-evidence with his work timesheets, which showed he was at work when those witnesses said he was abusing them. My mum told me on the phone that Davy often had forged timesheets done for him by a work colleague when he was on night shifts and how easy it was to get away with. She told me he often told his team he was in one place on the railway working on something, when in reality he would be at home or asleep in his van.

'Those girls are clear liars.' A man stopped me on the street near my mum's. 'It's very clear Davy has done nothing wrong.'

But I knew he had. Those people made me angry and I hated the system so much. I knew people would say the same about me if I went to court. I couldn't handle the idea of that at all.

The jury of his peers found Davy not guilty. He was acquitted. An innocent man in the eyes of the law, and that was so frustrating.

The average person doesn't understand how the courts work at all, so they come away believing that not guilty means innocent. Of course it doesn't, it just means the evidence wasn't enough. Juries are instructed to follow the guidelines to the letter and to acquit unless guilt is proved beyond a reasonable doubt. In a case like this, where there are only three witnesses and one of them is lying – or to use a phrase the press love, 'he said, she said' – it's never good for the victims. Someone's word against a reputable man like Davy Tweed might not always be believed. And in this case it wasn't. Soon people were approaching me saying that they knew he hadn't done anything and talking about 'those girls' as if describing a breed of animal. They said they knew it was all lies. They would repeat how Davy was not guilty, an innocent man.

'There is no smoke without fire,' I would respond every time.

I was angry that people didn't believe the witnesses. I was angry that it probably meant I would not be believed either. I was sad that there was no justice – not for the woman, not for Emma, not for me.

Mum applied for a restraining order for her and the kids, as we were terrified of what would happen now. Would Davy try to get back into the house? Would he be buoyed up by his victory and show aggression?

We went to court to get it, and my mum's solicitor read her statement out in front of me. Hearing it all put together – all the horrible, evil violence we had witnessed over the years – it seemed unbelievable that my mum was still alive at all. Some of the things that were in the statement were things I had not known, disgusting things that Davy Tweed did to my mum. They made my blood turn cold and I was really angry, a rage bubbling inside me for the entire time.

Something to be grateful for just then was the direction that social services had given my mum as soon as the allegations were made, to put Davy out. But there were symptoms of a broken system all the same. Even with the restraining order against him, my mum was told that she was the one who had to drop off and collect the girls from supervised visits with their father – if she didn't she would be in breach of the contact order and risked him getting custody of them! It seemed crazy to all of us.

I myself was feeling fairly guilty as well, wondering if I had made a statement would it have been something that would have ensured a different outcome. I wondered what would have happened if I had stood up in court and told my own story. I imagined it would have been a support to the allegations and the police had told me it would have helped.

I started suffocating myself with these thoughts, forcing myself to think about other outcomes and other verdicts. I took the weight of the not guilty verdict onto my shoulders and it started to crush me. Guilt is such a strange emotion, especially when you have low mental health anyway. You can really begin to despise yourself and feel like you are worthless. In my case I had nothing cohesive inside my mind, just a jumble of blame and all the fingers I imagined were pointing at me.

Despite my ability to give good advice, I was not able to apply the things I knew to myself. The small, hurt child inside me was doing what children do, looking inward to blame and shame. I hated myself. I started to dream about dying in an accident; I'd see visions of myself crashing down steps and falling from heights. I would lie in bed imagining the peace of death, when the constant ticking clock of my self-hatred would cease to be. I felt nothing but a dark cloak over me, blurring my vision, and it almost destroyed me.

Gavin grew increasingly concerned and frustrated by his inability to help me in any way. He started to panic, obviously recognising depression and suicidality when he saw it.

'I'd not survive without you, Amanda,' he would say, trying to get me to look at him, but I couldn't. I wasn't in the room, I was inside my head, lost, suffocating and absolutely devastated. I started binge drinking. Once a month I would go to the pub and get out of my head. The alcohol was an anaesthetic.

My husband, desperate for reasons to explain my behaviour, thought I was having an affair and questioned me. I was really irritated by that, and as I threw words at him, like "why don't you trust me" and "what's your problem", the cracks in my marriage and my world got wider.

Davy had been strutting around town since he was acquitted, drinking all the time with his so-called friends. I couldn't understand how anyone wouldn't have reservations about any person accused of molesting children. But it seems the not guilty verdict was enough to appease everyone in Davy's social and political circle.

It felt like he had won. It felt like people were eating out of his hand. He was seen drinking with young women – girls my age and younger. It was making me sick. I tried to speak to them and at one point I approached their mothers, but I was dismissed with a wave of their hands as if I was crazy, as if I was a liar.

My demons confronted and my worst fear realised – being turned away for blowing the whistle – changed something, and I remember driving with Gavin in the car just to get out of the house, he was so worried about me.

'Pull over,' I said.

He pulled in and turned the engine off. God knows what he thought I was going to say.

'The girls who accused Davy, they were telling the truth.'

'How do you know that?' He seemed confused. 'What's this about?'

'I know they're telling the truth because he did the same to me,' I said.

It felt as though my ribcage was wide open and my heart was beating in full view. When I say I started to cry I mean in the way children do, I opened my mouth and I roared. All the frustrations of twenty years of abuse and watching my mother beaten came out like a torrent. I sobbed until my lungs ached and my nose was raw and my eyes felt like they would close for a hundred years. My husband held me really tight.

'I don't know what to say,' he said. But I could feel his support as he rubbed my back and fixed the strands of hair wet from my tears.

'I want to go to the police,' I said. 'I feel so guilty, I wish I had gone before ... those poor girls being called liars and I know they're not.'

Gavin straightened up and took his embrace away. 'I don't know, Amanda,' he said, and the sympathy was gone from his tone. 'Maybe let sleeping dogs lie, no? I mean, do you want to be called a liar too?'

That felt comfortable and easy when he said it. A chance card.

But I knew that wasn't my road. I knew what my road was, it stretched out before me. It was the road I didn't take when I was four, five, seven, ten, fifteen, twenty. But it was a road I was setting out on right now.

I was going to tell on Davy Tweed. I was going to make a statement. I was going to tell the whole world.

16

Making a Statement

If I had told on Davy years ago, maybe other girls wouldn't have been hurt, but maybe they would. I couldn't know. All I could know is that I was feeling strong enough to do this and I would do it. I held that in my heart, like a letter to myself. You can do this Amanda, you must not be afraid.

'I'm going to tell, Mum,' I had said the day before. 'I'm going to go to the police about Davy.'

'Right,' she said, 'let me get my coat.' There she was again, the undying support, my rock. Still my lovely mum after years of battering and abuse. I wondered if I had told would she have left years ago – I believe she would have. He could convince her she deserved beatings, but he would never have convinced her to sacrifice us. No way.

'I'll call them first,' I said, and she sat there with me as I dialled the police station and spoke to the officer. I said what I was calling for, and who I was. They sent an unmarked car up to the house to collect me the next day and I went down to the station. My mum came with me. As we pulled in, the police officer driving looked over his shoulder and said, 'You ready to do this?'

'As ready as I'll ever be,' I said. I was not ready; how could I ever be ready? But it didn't matter. I had to do it and I had to do it now. I had to stop Davy from hurting anyone else in the way he hurt me and the others.

'I play rugby a bit myself,' the police officer said, 'I know Davy and his brother a bit.'

I caught my mum's eye, and we both shook our heads. We were up against it already.

'Come on,' my mum said and set her mouth in a hard line.

We walked into the station arm in arm.

'I don't have dates, I just know how old I was,' I said off the bat.

'Sure that's alright,' the policeman said, 'just tell me what you do remember.'

I stared him down.

'I was a wee child,' I said, 'I wasn't taking notes when I was being assaulted in my own home.'

He nodded, 'I understand.'

The verdict from the other case rang in my head like a bell. *Not Guilty. Not Guilty.*

'David Tweed is a paedophile,' I said quite loudly. I gripped the seat of my chair with both hands, 'whether the law says so or not!'

The policeman nodded, holding a pencil in his hand.

'If you're not going to act in my interest, I'll go to the ombudsman!' I said really loudly, feeling the pressure of his rugby connections.

'Amanda, I'm sorry, but do you think I'm not on your side here?' he said then.

'Youse shouldn't have a side,' I said, 'youse should be taking evidence.'

'I am,' he said and waved his pencil.

'The other girls who accused Davy ... I think youse let them down,' I said. 'Youse told everyone that a daughter had come forward and was protecting him, and now you're telling me you know him.'

'I do know him,' he said, 'but to be honest with you, the reason I was telling you that was just to be transparent. I actually really don't like Davy Tweed or his brother.'

'Well ... you should just do what you're supposed to,' I was flustered. My mum patted my arm. She understood.

So did the officer. 'Amanda, we are going to prosecute the person who has done you a great deal of harm. That's what's going to happen. We will arrest and charge him, and he will be prosecuted. That's all we can do.'

I calmed down. The policeman got me a bottle of water and sat silently while I pulled myself back from the ledge I'd just been standing on.

They took me into another room and left my mum waiting where she sat. 'When you're ready, Amanda, start at the very beginning,' the policeman said.

I don't know how long I was in that chair at that desk with that police officer. But when we left the station it was dark and I was absolutely exhausted. So was my mum, hours spent outside the door not knowing what was being said behind it.

I was wrapped in my big coat, but I was freezing. My mind was blank. It was as though I had left all of my memories inside there on the paper. The policeman had told me he would type up everything I had said and I could come back and read through it and add something if I wanted.

At Mum's, Lorraine was waiting with her little boy on her knee in the living room. I'd never told her, but I knew she knew.

'How did you get on?' she asked.

'It was good to get it out I suppose,' I said. 'I've done what I can now, to stop Davy.'

I should have known from how Lorraine was asking me so many questions that she was thinking of doing the same, but at that point I still thought it was just me who had suffered sexual abuse at Davy's hands. I should have realised when Lorraine asked me about every inch of the process I had just gone through in the station, but I just thought she was trying to be supportive.

When my mum dropped me home, the first thing I did was tell my husband that I had gone to the police.

'Was that the right thing to do, Amanda?' he said, looking down at the floor, his gaze fixed on one spot.

'Of course it was,' I said. 'I should have gone ages ago.'

'You know they'll call you a liar,' he said, 'like they did with those girls?'

'Don't say "those girls",' I said.

'Well, you know you'll get that treatment, don't you?' Gavin said.

'So what?' I raised my voice a little, 'I'm telling the truth – my truth – and people can say what they want about me, it won't change that it's true.'

I had a lump in my throat. I told myself that Gavin was just worried about me as his wife, about the pain that would come if my case went the way of the last one. And I have no doubt he was thinking of himself too – how he would want to defend me and how that might play out. But I didn't need that right then, I needed a hug and reassurance. I didn't need his first thoughts to be what other people would think. I needed to know what he thought, and I needed him to be on my side.

As I lay in bed that night thinking of the words on the page, I felt something was lighter. Had I left my pain on the paper? I doubted it.

The next day my phone rang.

'Amanda,' my mum's voice was urgent down the phone, 'can you come over? I need you to come here now.'

I had the dog on the lead, about to leave for a walk, when she called, so I just put the dog in the car and drove straight over. In the scenarios that I ran through my head on the drive, the reality was not included. But I knew what it was as soon as I went into the house, through the door my mum was already holding open and into the living room, where my sister Lorraine was sitting on the couch with red eyes.

I went straight down on my knees in front of her. 'What is it?'

But I knew.

She lifted her eyes to meet mine and we stared at each other for a minute.

'Me too,' was all she could say.

My mum was rigid, but I could see her thoughts racing behind her eyes. I knew her thoughts were riddled with guilt and a protectiveness that was too late.

We sat together, the three of us, saying the same things over and over. Telling each other we were sorry, that we should have known, that we should have said.

'I want to go to the police,' Lorraine said. 'I can't stand him walking around like a peacock, talking about the victims of his case as liars, when I know they're telling the truth.'

I nodded – I knew that feeling.

'Is it okay if I go to the police, Amanda, is it okay with you?' she asked.

I will admit my first instinct was to say no. I wanted the clock to rewind and turn back the time to when I was a child and I could have stopped all of this. I wanted to say no because I didn't want her to have to go through what I had gone through the day before. Giving a statement is such an invasion – all the things you've hidden deep inside being recorded on a lined page in such a clinical manner.

But I knew she had to do it. Because even though it was so hard, I had to do it too.

'Of course it's okay with me,' I said.

There was a flush through me of pain, real physical pain, at the thought that my sister, in this moment of revelation to me of her own tragedy, was worried that I would feel stress if she went to the police. It was so hard. I should have protected her. I knew what Davy was capable of. I had promised myself as a child that if he touched any one of my sisters I would tell on him. I felt like I failed in that promise, at least the little girl inside me who made it felt that. The woman I was then knew that I did my best, that I was not to blame. Cerebrally I knew the only person to blame was Davy, but I still felt such guilt.

The knowledge that Lorraine had been abused shattered the idea that I had had, which was that Davy had abused me because I wasn't his flesh-and-blood daughter. Now I didn't know how to feel. I realised it didn't matter either way to him, and it made me really angry. All those years I blamed myself, thinking it was because of me that he abused me. It wasn't. He would have abused any girl in his home, related, unrelated, visitor, friend.

Lorraine made her statement. We were told our complaints were to be taken seriously and would be sent to the public prosecution service together in one file. If it was considered strong enough to try Davy, then that would be done. We would just have to wait and see.

At this stage Davy was still getting visitations with his children. Every week my mum was forced by the law to bring her girls down to meet Davy, where he had full contact, with the only supervision being his sister. It was a failure of the system and of safeguarding. He took them to the cinema and sat in the dark with them. Every one of them complained about it, that they didn't want to go, but my mum was forced to bring them. One week Davy pulled Jamiee Leigh out of her seat as the movie played and onto his knee. My mum wanted to pull her back and cause a fuss, but she had been warned by the state not to interfere with Davy's visits or risk losing her children to him. A few moments later Jamiee-Leigh started to cry. My mum stood up and lifted her off her father's knee and took her outside. Jamiee Leigh told Mum that Davy was rubbing her on his leg and it hurt. My mum took her straight down to the police station.

'They said there isn't much they can do – sitting a child on his knee isn't enough,' my mum said to me down the phone.

'I can't believe you have to bring them down, after everything.' I was in shock. I could not believe that pervert had done something to his daughter in public. But he didn't know about our statements. It was almost as if getting an acquittal in the court case had made him feel like the world understood him, like his actions had no consequences and he was free to do as he liked.

'Have you spoken to Cat and Victoria?' I said to my mum and she went quiet, so I knew she had and I knew what they had said.

'I knew Cat hated her dad, but I thought it was because of how violent he was with us,' I said, 'and I just never thought he would lay a hand on them, I really didn't.'

'I never saw it and I'm their mum,' she said.

'I wish so much I asked them years ago,' I said to fill the silence.

'You were dealing with your own abuse,' she said.

'So were you, Mum,' I said.

17

Searching for Peace

I'm not sure when Davy found out there was another case against him, and I'm not sure when he found out that it was us. But he started turning up everywhere. If I was walking out of work, I'd see him drive by, and he would slow down and glare out the window at me. The minute I saw his car I would feel like I was a child again, and I mean it when I say it was scary. I knew of violence against women firsthand, and he was capable of it. I really believe to this day that Davy Tweed was capable of murder. I think he came seriously close to it a few times with my mum.

It seemed Davy was timing these drive-bys because he knew when I was leaving work. So I started waiting in work until other people were also leaving, and then I'd go, feeling safety in numbers.

'Do any of us even know him?' My colleague saw with her own eyes Davy slow down and stare at us.

'It's my mum's ex-husband,' I said.

'What a weirdo,' she said, 'what does he want?'

'To scare me.' I was honest.

You tell on me and I will kill you.

Every day without fail Davy Tweed would make sure I saw him. And it was working. I was so stressed out that I considered retracting my statement. Maybe my husband was right, this was something I couldn't handle.

I wasn't safe. I knew that to the core of my being.

I needed to speak to someone who wasn't involved with any of this on any level. I needed to fully express myself and speak from my heart and mind. So I signed up to a free counselling service in Belfast. But it would be a while until I could get an appointment.

One day I was in the supermarket, grabbing a sandwich for my lunch on my break from work, and I saw the reverend. The one I had walked out on during his sermon in our church. I saw him and he saw me – his eyebrows flashed up and down with that unmistakable expression of recognition. I attempted to leave, but he called me by name and followed up with, 'How is your mother now?'

'Fine,' I said.

'Why did your mother tell her husband to move out?' There was no beating around the bush with this man. He had not spoken to my mum about any of this and neither had he offered her any support, even though she was the one who attended church weekly – Davy never, ever did.

'Reverend,' I said, 'with all due respect, if you're wanting to know personal things like that you'll have to ask my mum.'

'I am simply asking how she is,' he said.

'You're looking for gossip,' I said, 'and you won't get any from me.'

'I'm concerned,' he said.

'Reverend, I know you notice when people don't show up for church,' I said. 'I know that because you noticed when I didn't. I also know you have our phone number.'

He frowned at me, 'I do.'

'So my mum is missing from your church for weeks and you don't call once?'

This time it was me who shook my head and wagged my finger at him. I turned on my heel and went to the till. Paying for my sandwich with shaking hands I looked back, but he was gone.

Since making the statement the new memories had continued to pop up and they were pulling me down. I don't know if you have ever felt real regret, but it feels like a gnawing ache that makes your mind race and your throat hurt. How could this be the way it is? How could I have stayed silent for so many years and suffered so much when I was saving no one at all when it came to it? I didn't feel like I could talk to my mum or Lorraine about my darkest feelings. We were all blaming ourselves for what happened to each other.

Davy was stalking me and harassing me, and I felt this immense regression to fear. I cannot explain it, but it overrode my ability to think straight. When I told Gavin that Davy was stalking me, standing outside my job, driving by, he said that I knew what I was getting into. That made me feel so alone.

One day I noticed Davy standing across the road. His head was down and he was staring at me from under his eyebrows. I wanted him to feel how he was making me feel, so, as I chatted there with my colleagues, I made a joke and pointed at Davy, and of course they all looked over and every one of them was laughing. The joke wasn't about him, but it worked – he felt intimidated and walked off. He had lost his power in that moment and he knew it.

I didn't see him much after that. The worm had turned.

Finally, I got my appointment for counselling. The waiting room was a library of pamphlets advertising services for mental health, sexual health and for victims of domestic abuse or sexual violence. I think I read every one of those leaflets while I waited.

The room where I met with the counsellor was so plain it surprised me. There were two red tub chairs and a brown coffee table, with a box of tissues on my side and nothing else.

I didn't talk about abuse in that space at first, even though she knew about it as it was written plainly on my form. She asked me what was on my mind and I told her everything but that. I chatted about my life in general, about the comings and goings of my husband and my married life. Eventually we came to the pass, where I had to mention what had gone on. I told her about my guilt, and I cried and cried.

'You are looking at this through the lens of an adult mind,' she said to me. 'A child's mind sees differently, you cannot judge yourself like this.'

'I feel like I could have ... I should have done something.'

'You did what you had to do to survive,' she said.

'But I'm not surviving,' I said.

She discussed my weight with me and we talked about how thin I was and why. I wasn't fully honest, as starving myself was one thing I controlled and I didn't want to be open about it.

I thought about leaving Gavin and running away from all of this. I thought about changing my name and starting over somewhere new. I imagined lying still with no thoughts in my head at all. I imagined how darkness would feel if there was never light. It was the only option that made me feel better. I decided I wanted out.

I planned my suicide to the smallest detail. I tidied up a few loose ends so that there wouldn't be difficulties afterwards for people, but not enough that anyone would notice. I organised the photographs and the clothes and my jewellery. And I wrote a letter listing what was there and what was to be given to my sisters and my cousins, and why.

I didn't want anyone to find me when I ended things. I just wanted to disappear. I decided that if I was ever to be found dead, it would need to be by the police or someone who didn't know me. I thought through the idea that I wouldn't succeed, that things would go wrong. I knew I had to make sure first time. I decided to distance myself from everyone I loved. I would push them away. I started to tell my husband that he could do better than me, I told him he deserved better. I told him I didn't think he was happy and I said I knew I was dragging him down. Where I could, I withdrew.

'Till death do us part' was the vow I had taken. In the dark of the night I knew I was doing the right thing.

I had written other letters by this stage. Long explanations of why I was dead and how sorry I was about everything. I wrote them with tears streaming down my face, at times sobbing so hard I had to stop. The paper was stained with my tears. I hid them in the back of the dresser, where I knew Gavin wouldn't look. I planned to stop in the shop on my way to end everything, to get stamps there and post them on the way to my chosen location.

As the days went on it felt like I was getting closer to the door out of here. By a certain stage I felt like I had my hand on the handle of the door and I was ready to turn it. I felt so light and so good for the first time in my life.

In my letters I had expressed my deepest regrets and I apologised to each person for failing them as much as I had. I was so lightheaded with the joy of my escape plan that I was lighthearted in the messages. I joked with Gavin about finding a new wife and how easy it would be for him being such a young, handsome widower. I said I was sorry we had not had a baby; I was sorry he had nobody to carry on his name. I knew that if we had ever had a baby, I would never go like this, but I was glad I could. I didn't want to stay. I couldn't stay.

But it hurt still, to know I would never grow old, I would never see my sisters grow old either, I wouldn't see them get married. I cried when I realised I would not walk Buster again. I said goodbye to him; he already knew my plans. I told him about everything on our walks together.

'Buster, I have such a burden, I can't do it,' I said, 'I need peace, I need sleep.'

My plan was set for a Friday. I had every step managed and I knew where I was going.

Then my phone rang.

At the time that everything was happening with the statements to the police and with Davy, Jamiee-Leigh wasn't at all well. My littlest sister is diabetic. She has been since she was five, when we noticed her behaving oddly – like she was drunk – and brought her to the hospital. She was giggling at random things and swaying like she'd had five pints. We had been out shopping, getting a few groceries, when this started, and at first we thought she was joking, maybe copying someone or something she had seen. We had popped her into the shopping trolley because she was being so erratic. It took us a while to figure out something was really wrong.

By now her diabetes was becoming very hard to manage, even though she was a great girl with it, remembering what she could have and what she couldn't. She controlled her diet as she was told and never missed her insulin. But she is a 'brittle diabetic', which means that her glucose levels swing from one extreme to another. It's very hard to control.

'Amanda,' I could hear my mother sobbing on the other end.

'Is it Jamiee-Leigh? Mum! Who is it?' I knew someone was ill or worse, dead.

She didn't speak for a few moments, as she pushed her sobs back down and swallowed them. 'Amanda ...' she said, 'It's ... It's ...'

'Mum are you at the hospital? I'm coming down!'

The phone was taken from her and I heard my sister Catherine's voice.

'It's Susan, Mo. She's dead,' she said.

Susan? My aunt? She was only forty-nine and in full health.

I asked so many questions, but all Catherine said was, 'She killed herself.'

My initial thoughts were selfish, but I was really annoyed. My plans were set; now I would have to rethink. How could I possibly commit suicide this week when Susan had beaten me to it? Those are the thoughts of the severely depressed. The state my mum was in over her sister, there was no way I could add to that.

My mum came back on the line.

'Amanda, can you drive me up to see her, when I get back from the hospital?'

'Of course I can.' My selfish thoughts dissipated and now I just wanted to be there with my family and take in the news that my lovely aunt was dead.

'Can you ring Daddy?' Mum said.

I said I would, but I was sad about doing it. My grandfather had only just started to get used to life without his beloved wife, my granny. 'A child should never die before the parent,' he said over and over again. It was one of the saddest calls I've ever made.

Gavin offered to come home early from work, but I told him not to. In fairness, I wasn't at all attached to my emotional side at that time, I was barely crying. I have always had a hard time being emotional or expressing my feelings; sometimes I feel like I don't feel the way other people do. Back then, I was cold and really detached, like I had no emotions at all. I told people what had happened as if it was something trivial, something everyday. My aunt had lost her battle with depression and killed herself and to me it was an inconvenience. That is how hollow I had become. From the outside I looked fine, I smiled and chatted with friends, but that was a shell. Inside there was darkness, bad feelings and a plan to destroy myself.

In the wake of Susan's death what I was thinking about was how long it would be acceptable to leave it until I killed myself. Would a week be long enough? Probably not. Maybe a month. It felt so long. I wanted to go now.

I spent the next few days going through the motions, organising things for my mum and attending the funeral, but once the funeral was over, I was left with this anger because that was my day when

I should have been freed. And I was still here.

I could only give this a few weeks, I thought. I have to go. I have to.

When that final Friday came, I texted my mum to check she was going to Belfast that day, and when she said she was, I asked if I could come along. I only took my handbag, a pair of clean underwear, my hairbrush and my straighteners. I left my toothbrush, so as not to give Gavin any cause to notice that. It would have concerned him. I texted him to say I was going to Belfast, hugged my dog goodbye and told him I would see him in heaven. I told him I loved him but had to go. It was so sad, and I cried my eyes out saying goodbye. Then I composed myself, said goodbye to my mother-in-law, and got into my mother's car knowing I was never coming back.

The finality of that thought put me in good form, and as we drove I looked out the window at everything passing by, knowing this would be the last time I would pass there. There were no alarm bells – I was quiet, but nobody looking at me would have seen anything but a light heart.

I went with my mum to see my grieving Granda, and then we went down to see my Aunt Carla.

Then the time came to go home.

'Right,' said my mum pressing her hands onto her knees to stand up, 'we better go before it gets too dark.'

'I'm not going home mum,' I said.

Everyone looked at me.

'What do you mean you're not going home?' my mum said. 'Where are you going then?'

'You can stay here,' Carla said.

'Naw,' I said, 'I'm not going home, I can't. I just need to be away; I have to go.'

The quiet room was filled with the sound of beating hearts as my mum read between the lines and knew exactly what I meant when I said that.

'Why don't you come home with me?' she said cheerily, but I could hear the panic. 'We can talk and you can tell me what's been going on.'

'Nothing's going on,' I said. 'I'm not going home, I'm going.'

I was talking in riddles, but the context was clear. Everyone in that room could hear my cries for help, even if I didn't know I was screaming so loudly.

My aunt stood up beside my mother.

'Amanda,' was all she said. My mother put her hand in front of her sister.

'Amanda,' she said too, and she was breathing really frantically, 'you come home with me now and we can sort all of this out.'

'No,' I said. 'Gavin will convince me to go back home, nothing will change, my life won't get better. It's over. I need to just go now away, by myself.'

'Did you tell him you're leaving?' My mum's tone was softer but still concerned.

I shook my head.

'Ring him now,' she said.

'Not yet, I'll speak to him soon,' I replied.

'You better, Amanda. This isn't really the way to do things. What am I supposed to tell him if he calls up to my house looking for you?'

'You won't have to tell him anything, he won't call to yours, I'll talk to him.'

'Right, well, are you okay?' Mum asked.

'No! But I will be,' I said.

She hugged me and left.

'Yay, you can come out with me this weekend for my mate's birthday!' my cousin said.

'Yeah, sure,' I replied.

Nobody had known this was coming, nobody was expecting this. I wasn't either. I wasn't expecting to have to do this, and it wasn't about my marriage or my relationship with Gavin and everything to do with survival.

I went up to my aunt's spare bedroom to speak to my husband. I sat with my phone in my hand not knowing how to explain this, what to say, was this over? Did I need to break up with him in order to try to survive all of this? I didn't know. My heart ached. It broke for how much I knew this would hurt him. It broke because as much as I loved him, I couldn't live that life anymore. It broke because this meant that I was losing my best friend. But I knew I had to find a way of surviving and I knew if I had continued as I was, I would have ended up dead and I couldn't hurt my mum or my sisters like that.

At that, my phone pinged. It was a text message from him asking when I would be home.

I replied, 'I am not coming home tonight.' In that moment I thought that maybe I should just rip this plaster off and be done with it. I couldn't have him holding on until I was well enough to go back because that wouldn't be fair on him. He needed a clean break so he could get over it and move on. He deserved more. I loved him too much to keep hurting him like this.

My phone pinged again. 'Okay, what's happened, when will you be home?'

'Probably not ever.' I paused, then I hit send.

I sat with my phone in my hand waiting for a response. I felt a bit lighter now that this had been done. But I didn't feel good about it. My heart raced and I felt lightheaded. I guess I was holding my breath without realising.

Hours passed and I had no response from him. I figured maybe these past few months he was hoping for this anyway but didn't want to do it himself. I went to bed with my phone in my hand. Waiting for a response that never came, I began to cry. Eventually, exhausted from the crying, I fell asleep. It was the first time in months that I had slept more than two hours.

I woke feeling slightly refreshed, until I remembered all that had happened and then my heart shattered all over again. My aunt called in to see if I was awake and if I wanted any breakfast. I wasn't eating, I didn't want to eat – I felt sick. I felt terrible about what I had just done. I knew I had broken his heart and it made me feel like the worst person ever. I never wanted to hurt him like this.

My cousin came in to see if I was okay and talk about how long I had planned on staying there. Indefinitely, I think, I didn't know. She suggested that we go shopping for some supplies and clothes to do me. I needed toiletries and underwear and some clothes, so we went to the Abbey Centre.

The whole time I held my phone tightly in my hand, so I didn't miss a call or a text from him. I knew he would be at football but wondered if maybe he would message me just before or after. The day passed and night came – still nothing. I was afraid to call or text him in case he was angry with me. He had every right to be. I'm sure he hated me. I hated me for what I had just done.

18

Barely Surviving

When a week had passed and I hadn't heard from Gavin, a strange thing happened. Maybe it was reverse psychology at play, but I had left him and yet now I found myself staring at my phone waiting for a call or text. I started yearning for his arms around me, and I will be honest, I missed him. I mean I married him for good reason. He always made me laugh, he had a way of being really silly and it just got me in the funny bone. He would do this thing where he would sing a couple of lines of a popular song but would sing off-key, dreadfully and really loud, and no matter what was going on I would find myself instantly in better form, laughing. I started to crave our little living room, with us two sitting on the floor playing video games in complete darkness, crying out or shouting and groaning as we lost, or whooping as we won. I thought about how fun that was, and I really missed it, and I missed myself. Where had I gone? I had become this dark brooding shell of a person, with plans to end it all. Why? How had that happened to me?

I wanted to go back.

But I stayed at my aunt's. I deleted every social media account I owned and I hid in her spare room, behind dark curtains that stopped the sunshine from reaching me. I didn't want to see it. I wanted no reminder that there were good things in the world. I was out of control, pushing my own head underwater with the frustration of a life I hadn't asked for. I had no concept of what was real and what was not – if my mind was playing games or if my thoughts were sincere. I felt heartbroken, but I couldn't figure out for what. I mean my life with my husband was what I had run from, right?

When I hear the word turmoil, I think of that time. When you feel upside down and you go from A to Z and back without even knowing what you think about either. It's like existing in a whirlpool. Not only are you drowning, but you're being thrown about as well.

Because of where I was living then, I was able to reconnect with some people I used to work with. I was deliberately attempting to fake 'normal' so I could maybe swing myself back into it for real. Some of them were people I had believed were real friends, who knew Gavin too. I met him in school; we were friends the whole way along and I suppose people thought it was very romantic that we ended up together. They could see, even though I tried to cover it up, that I was struggling, and some of them presumed it was the breakup. And I suppose it was, in a way.

'Why not give him a ring? Go for a drink and a chat,' was one suggestion.

'Just go over and tell him you want to make it work,' was another.

I fantasised that my husband would be the one to come to find me. I imagined him arriving at the house and coming in, out of breath from running all the way there. I dreamed of him scooping me up in his arms and announcing we were running away to Australia.

Those fantasies helped me understand that it wasn't him I was running from, it was Ballymoney. The town where I had suffered my childhood was the prison I wanted to escape from.

I contacted my manager in the bank I worked at in Ballymoney and asked her advice on getting a transfer. I wanted to work at any other branch of the bank but that one. She said she would contact head office and put the transfer request through on my behalf. I wanted to work, I liked working, but I could not continue centring my life in that small town. It was barely five kilometres from one end to the other, and Davy Tweed was all over it.

I wanted my life, I did. But I wanted my life out of there.

It was as if the universe heard me. My phone pinged in my pocket and I saw my husband's name on the screen. I was so glad that he was letting his guard down. I presumed the text would be about meeting up, working things out, all the things I had in my head. But it wasn't.

'Sorry it's taken me this long to reply to you, but I was so angry Amanda. I still am.'

I sat down.

The text continued.

'I don't know what has gone wrong or what I did. You've been off for months. Is there someone else?'

I stared at that line: Is there someone else? How could he be so blind to what I had been going through?

The text finished with, 'I don't even know if I want to hear back from you, I'm still angry and hurt.'

I read the message over and over again. It wasn't the romantic reprieve I had hoped for. Of course it wasn't, this was real life not a movie. Looking back now I had definitely romanticised Gavin instead of thinking of him as the man I knew. But I was really sorry that he was so hurt he didn't want to talk to me, that felt terrible. I hadn't thought of that. I'd been so consumed with my own pain that I didn't consider the fact that I was causing so much. I knew, of course, if I died he would have been hurt, but I thought he would get over it. What I had written in the letter about him finding someone else quickly was how I saw it.

I was very sure that I didn't want to be honest with Gavin at any point. If I told him, or anyone, just exactly how I was thinking, I'd have been put into hospital, and I didn't want that. I didn't want to be managed; I wanted the freedom I had here.

I wrote back to him. I told him there was nobody else, I said I was sorry and I wanted him to be happy.

'Why else would you leave like that?' came the response. 'There must be someone else, everyone is saying it.'

Everyone is saying it? I did not like that at all. Who exactly was 'everyone' anyway? Not one of our mutual friends had so much as checked on me since I left. It was as if I didn't exist.

'Who is saying that?' I texted back. I wanted to know. I was really annoyed because it was so typical that cheating was the only reason a woman could leave her situation. So nobody wondered if I was unhappy, or if he was making me unhappy? They just jumped to the first conclusion – that I was clearly the bad one in this equation. It was unfair.

'Everyone. My parents, our friends, everyone is saying it, that I shouldn't trust you.'

I felt like I had been punched in the gut. I had been a good wife and a good daughter-in-law, and I was a good friend. I realised right then that I had no friends in that circle, I was nothing more than an accessory in my husband's life, and when things went wrong it would have to be my fault. They couldn't see past the end of their noses in that small town, to imagine a scenario where I was the one in trouble. No. The scarlet letter was pinned to my chest the moment I left. I could see that clearly. They wrote me off with bad minds and bad intent the minute I made Gavin unhappy.

They knew nothing about me.

I was glad I left then, and I'm glad I left now, even though those were the darkest, most confused days of my whole life. Maybe it was that town, but it was clear to me that nobody there cared much about me at all. None of them supported me, and I think that is mostly why I was so depressed. Those little side eyes and questions like 'Would you not let sleeping dogs lie?' When at the end of the day I was the victim of a heinous crime – one that threads depression into the fibre of your being.

I spent a while after the text conversation ranting to myself.

'Tell your family and friends they know nothing about me to be spreading lies and gossip!' I wrote after an hour.

'They're just saying it because I'm so hurt,' he replied.

'Well tell them I said thanks for the support!'

I threw my phone down into my open bag and burst into tears. I did believe that people were saying that to him. It made sense that they would, because they were small-minded and ignorant. Nobody could imagine that my life with my husband could be bad, because I was a woman and women should be grateful for having a husband at all. They didn't care that I had been so down, even though they had seen it. I was at the point of killing myself, doing the worst thing imaginable, and all they could find in their brains were accusations of bad behaviour. I had spent so much time with my parents-in-law and in the company of my so-called friends, but it turned out they didn't know me at all.

I got petty. I reactivated all of my social media just to delete everyone I knew from that town. Every single person from Ballymoney was defriended, unfollowed, blocked. I did not and would not trust even one of them. Screw them all.

I moved in with an old friend who was looking for a housemate. While they were at work I sat staring at the wall. I would fake normal when they came back, slapping a smile on my face and chatting back. At weekends I put on a happy face and went to the bar with her and our mutual friends from school.

To be honest that friendship and living in that house saved me. I started eating better and being good to myself. My friends kept me going. I can't explain it, but the female company, this pressure-free environment where I wasn't expected to be good, where I wasn't expected to put someone else before myself, where I wasn't a servant – it was medicine. When we went out, I could leave my depression at the house, in my room. Like a packed bag, it stayed there until I came back. I didn't forget about it, I knew it was back there and would always be, but I could leave it and have fun. With these women I had a chance to be okay.

Months went by this way, weekdays sitting in my room waiting, evenings chatting or walking to the bar, weekends going for lunch or into town. My mum was at me to go to the doctor. 'Come on now, you're depressed, Amanda. It's not good to try to sort it yourself,' she said.

But I didn't go, and I didn't want to go to counselling either. To be honest, what I wanted was just to exist. I wanted to just be. I wanted my thoughts, my memories and my pain. I wanted to struggle this much, I wanted to find it hard to get to the end of each day. It felt appropriate to me. How else could I learn to live with what I had been through? If I didn't walk back through the battlefield, how could I learn what way I could better fight next time? I knew I had terrible mental health, but in a weird way the darkness fit the trauma I was moving through. I wanted to feel it. I wanted to feel all of my history and that was how I could get over it. This wasn't just a broken bone or a cut. This was a broken child figuring out how to be a whole woman again.

Sometimes I regretted so much that I was still here. Sometimes I would feel so pointless and wish I'd just gone to that abandoned house I knew about and been done with all of this. But I just couldn't do it to my mother. I knew she knew it was on my mind, she was so panicked about getting me to talk to the GP and take medications. I didn't feel like I could give her that regret, that guilt. Because I lived with that myself and it was too much.

One evening I was watching TV with my housemate and on the local news I saw Davy. His Ulster Unionist Coalition Party member William Wilkinson had been tried and found guilty of rape, and they had sentenced him to time in prison.

'Like attracts like,' I muttered.

That left Davy alone in his party. I suppose he could call himself party leader, but it was a party of one. It looked like it might be a humiliation. I looked at him on the screen, his red face sneering into the camera, and I wanted to smash it. He was there acting the big man still, while I was dying inside and barely existing in this life of depression.

I was drowning and he was standing on the bow of a ship heading into the sun.

How did he live like this? How was he not tormented by the memories of the things he had done? How was the sight of his own bare hands not reminding him of the punches he had landed on my mum? When he shook hands in the council, was he not reminded of the times he had my mother's neck in his fingers? When he looked at himself in the mirror, how was he not ashamed of the paedophile that stared back at him?

Davy thought he was untouchable because the community, his world, had told him he was not guilty. He had done the crime of course, so that made him feel invincible.

'I wish you would just fuck off and die,' I said to the TV.

Not long after that I got word that my transfer to the bank in Belfast had been approved. I was getting back into a routine and it felt good. My friends took me out to celebrate my new job and one of them arrived with a friend, Joe, who he said was at a loose end.

'The more the merrier,' I said.

For whatever reason, maybe the company, I had a really good laugh, to the point that my cheeks hurt. I hadn't felt like that in so, so long. I remember thinking, could this feeling come back for good? Could I feel happy again? Sitting outside the bar in the sun, I chatted and giggled and made jokes, and smiled so much. I wished you could get that on prescription, that feeling. I wished they made it.

My little sister Catherine and my cousin Gemma were grown up now, almost adults. I started to join them on nights out, getting addicted to the laughter and dancing that they brought with them to clubs and pubs. I felt normal more times than I felt depressed.

I'm not sure if it was that year, but there was a heavy snow. On my way back from work, desperate for something light and fun, I stopped at the shop and bought two pairs of welly boots. When I got down the road I saw Gemma.

'Come here!' I said waving the boots and she waved back. She gingerly made her way over, arms wide to avoid slipping.

When she got to me, she clung on to my arm and we tried walking together, ending up laughing our heads off like two baby deer on the ice.

'Let's go on holiday,' Gemma said, 'this cold doesn't suit us.'

I didn't need to think about it. A week in the company of people I loved, having fun? That was a no-brainer. I could feel the benefit of the holiday to my mental health just from deciding where to go.

We decided on Tunisia, and by the time we booked it we had collected family members like points in a video game. There were twelve of us going: my mum and all of my sisters, my nephew, and Uncle Danny and his wife, his daughter Gemma and his other kids.

We had a great time. Tunisia was so beautiful and where we were, in Monastir, was peaceful during the day but at night transformed into party central. I loved it. We went out every night, getting our glad rags on and doing our make-up and hair. It had been a long time since I had felt good about myself in a feminine way, and on that holiday with the sun on my skin and a genuine smile on my face I felt great. My sister Lorraine was on the holiday, but because she had a baby son, she was going to bed early, while the three singletons – me, Gemma and Cat – went out dancing all night long. I remember asking my uncle to take a photo of us and as he went to take it he called us 'three monkeys'. Instinctively the three of us formed the famous trio of hear no evil, see no evil, speak no evil. I covered my ears, Cat put her hands on her eyes and Gemma covered her mouth. We loved that picture so much. But when you think about everything in the context of our family and what came out, it's also really sad.

Not long after that Gemma told us that Davy had abused her too.

19

Life Goes On

My days were getting easier and my texts to Gavin were changing. We had gone from being frustrated, angry and upset, to being lighter, casual and even loving.

'You seem like your old self these days,' he texted one night.

'I feel like my old self,' I replied.

We decided to meet up.

My friends told me I would be fine. They gave me ways out and exits, and said they'd text and I could get them to call with an emergency if I wanted out. They helped me pick an outfit, do my hair and make-up, and they waved me off. Walking to meet him gave me butterflies, an excitement I hadn't felt in years and years. My step was light and I shook my hair off my shoulders when I saw him walk towards me. I smiled and he smiled too. After all this time it was really good to see him.

I told him that I had overloaded my mental health. I didn't want to tell him just how low I had got, I kept that to myself. I didn't want to fight, so I didn't talk him through how it felt to have so little support. I didn't tell him that I felt alone in my fight against Davy and that I felt he was on the other side from me ... and that Davy was on that side too so it was hard to cope.

Instead, we talked about the court case. He went a little hard on the side of caution, telling me again that I should think about how it would feel to be called a liar. He hadn't changed, he still didn't support me.

There was so much to consider and to be honest, even though I was feeling so much better, deep thought was an area I avoided. I couldn't stop thinking about Susan, and how close I had come to being where she was now. I felt so deeply sorry for her, how she felt in her last moments – I got it; I knew. The thoughts I had had in the aftermath of her death haunted me. How could I have been so selfish as to feel annoyed at her for dying first? How could I have felt bitter that she took my escape away? In so many ways, I know that if Susan hadn't done what she did, I would not be here today. It's a really hard idea to manage well, and sometimes I can't get it out of my head.

It was months after Susan died that I started to grieve for her. I don't know if I will ever stop, frankly. Her death is such a marker in my life and symbolises so much.

Gavin and I were at a stalemate. We had decided at our meet-up to see how things went, but I think both of us had already moved on in our heads. I don't want to even come close to telling you what I think his true reasons were, it wouldn't be fair. And mine were so jumbled that even now I can barely make them out. But at the end of it we found an excuse in the fact that I wouldn't move back to Ballymoney and he wouldn't move away. I didn't want to live near people who hadn't cared if I lived or died when I left my husband. And so, among all of the deeper reasons that meant we failed at being married to one another, my struggles with depression and his inability to be the man I needed, that small seemingly insignificant factor – where we would live – cemented our break-up as final. We were finished.

Gemma had been to the police and spoken to them about the abuse she remembered. It wasn't enough to make a case. They were sorry, but the memories she had were blurry and childish and she couldn't make head nor tail of them herself, except for the deep hurt of being sexually assaulted by someone you trust when you don't even understand the world around you.

I always describe childhood abuse as memories that make themselves known like pieces of a jigsaw flung out of the box. There is nothing more, a lot of the time, than snippets of memories, weird flashes of happenings that haunt you and frighten you, but you don't know what those are. So you can't talk about it, not really, because you don't know what the complete picture is of. You just know small pieces of it.

Gemma really wanted to be heard, but because of how the police were at that time, with no trauma officers, she was in effect silenced. They told her that her statement would not be added to a file against Davy. She felt the pressure of that more deeply than any of us recognised at that time. That would come to be another regret I have to live with, unfortunately.

There were now eight little girls who had been abused by Davy that we knew of. Emma and the woman who came forward at that time, myself, my four sisters and Gemma. Every one of us was dealing with bad mental health, every one of us was suffering and struggling to make sense of what had happened to us. All of us were being stared at, talked about, pointed at, called liars.

Nobody seemed to be pointing at Davy. Nobody was crushing

his will to live, nobody was hounding him or harassing him. Nobody was making his life difficult. In fact, from what we could see, he was being patted on the back more than pointed at, he was being applauded as a great man. I think, at least for me, that was the worst part about it.

I got a call from the policeman who had interviewed me. It was a simple call. He needed some more information for the case that they were preparing for the public prosecutor. There was going to be a court hearing, he said.

At first I was really glad to hear things were moving on. I never regretted making my statement as I felt that being involved with this case was the only thing I could do. But that didn't make it easy. It was hard to focus on anything without my thoughts going that way. I imagined an acquittal over and over again, imagined Davy's face, smug, red and fat, sneering at me. I imagined him coming to my house, barging in and beating me like he did my mum. I dreamed I woke up in the middle of the night to find his shadow over my bed.

My feeling side became quiet again – a recognisable numbness I knew to be a depressive episode. It was almost as though the curtains drew around me again.

Even so life went on. My grandad died of a heart attack, and we held a funeral. People talked about how great a man he was and Uncle Danny put a baby bottle of VAT19 rum in his jacket pocket as he lay in the coffin. I don't remember feeling much about that, I just went through the motions.

My cousin Gemma had her eighteenth birthday and we surprised her with my sister Catherine, who was in college in England. She hid in the car boot and then popped out of it outside the house, starting the night with real excitement for everyone. I danced with my family and friends all night, smiling and joking, but I felt like a puppet on a string, making all the right moves and expressions, but with nothing inside at all. I'd see men in the bars at the weekends, with their rugby shirts pulled over their fat bellies, and I'd feel like I just couldn't get away from Davy Tweed. The smallest thing would feel like an omen – he was going to get away with it, he was going to be acquitted and I would be lost to this feeling forever.

Back in my mum's house, with a few drinks in us, we found ourselves opening up a little.

'I hate him,' Gemma said, and she burst into tears.

'I hate him as well,' I said, 'I get it.'

'I can't even tell you what he did,' she said, 'it hurts too much to say it.'

'I get that as well.'

'Sometimes I feel like nobody believes me,' she said.

'I believe you,' I said looking her dead in the eye.

'The feelings I get from those memories,' Gemma said then, 'I don't think I can live with them.'

'I know what you mean,' I said then. But later on I would learn that I didn't.

I woke up in the early hours to the sound of my phone. I didn't answer. I was scared of who it was, and I thought I would just take a minute and then call the person back. Then came the ping of a voicemail. I dialled in.

The sounds of traffic and breathing at first gave me a start, but then a voice slurred into the phone. It was Joe, my boss's friend.

'Juswonderin … eh … if you'd ever be up for a date?' he said, then mumbled something before the call cut off.

I was really surprised by it, and amused. But I was also touched. We had had such fun when we first met, and that lunch was a moment I kept going back to, to remind myself that the real me was in there somewhere.

Given the time I'd had the missed call I replied, 'Ask me when you're sober!'

I didn't expect a reply, but I got one straight away.

'Okay I will,' it said.

I laughed and didn't know if this was fully serious, but I knew I wanted to go.

As soon as the morning came, literally at ten o'clock, my phone rang.

'Hello?' This was … interesting.

There was a pause, and I heard him clear his throat. 'Sorry about the voicemail,' he said.

'That's alright.' I let him off the hook.

'So …' he said, 'about that date … you on?'

I laughed. I liked this man. 'You sure you're sober?' I said.

'One hundred per cent sober and on my way to work.'

I pretended to think about it.

'Well, what do you think?' he said.

'Sure, I've nothing else on at the minute,' I said. I made him laugh.

'Thanks for clearing space in such a busy diary,' he said. 'I'll call you later, arrange something …'

I had never been on a proper date. My husband and I got together organically in school, growing closer in a shared group of friends in Ballymoney. He had never asked me out at all. This was like the movies – I would have to get myself ready and get picked up or meet him out. I was really excited.

Laughter really is the best medicine, I can attest to that. One date became two, became three and four, and suddenly we were seeing each other nearly every night. I was addicted to my good humour. I really loved how lighthearted and funny life seemed when I was with Joe. And I could see I was making him happier too.

A few dates in, I told him about the court case that was coming up. I told him the story. I think I wanted him to make the decision in regard to whether this budding relationship was coming at the wrong time. I wanted him to decide if it was too much, rather than consider that myself.

'And when is it?' he said when I finished.

I told him I didn't know. Then I told him the charge.

He took it in, but I saw his face fall, and he shook his head and really looked at me, right into my eyes.

'You're really brave,' he said. 'That would be hugely scary, facing someone like that in court.'

'It is,' I said, 'I'm dreading it.'

'Well look, Amanda,' he said, 'and I mean this, I'm here to support you. Even if these dates don't lead to the kiss I'm hoping for, I'll come with you.'

I remember drinking from my glass of wine and staring at my food, pushing it around the plate with my fork. It was the first time I felt that I had someone in my corner in the way that other people did. Sure, I had my mum and my sisters, but they were in this battle too, I couldn't lean on them, I couldn't hand them my gloves and ask for a minute. At that moment I didn't know if the man across from me was just Joe, or my friend, but it didn't matter. What he said, that he would be there, was the exact thing I really needed.

Up till then I realised that I had always put other people first, but the thing was so did they. I put my husband first and worried what the court case would be like for him. And that's normal. The problem was, he didn't do the same. He thought about himself too – there were two of us in that marriage worrying about his feelings and his state of mind.

When I lifted my eyes back to meet Joe's, my heart skipped a beat. I told myself that no matter what happened between us, that moment meant the world to me. I felt heard, I felt seen, I felt human.

The fact that a stranger could show more care to me than my husband or my friends ... it blew my mind. I immediately convinced myself this man was different. Even if I had never seen Joe again, I would have left that café with a new sense of self and what I deserved.

I did see him again though. There is such ease when you click with someone. I didn't feel pressure or try to be cool, I just went with what he suggested and we saw each other most days after work. It felt like we had always been together, that's how easy it was to be around each other.

In my eyes Joe kept proving himself, as my family continued to experience crisis after crisis. I ignored the red flags. My youngest sister's diabetes took a turn for the worse and she ended up in hospital in a diabetic coma. She was in the hospital in Ballymoney, and since I had moved back to Belfast, I had really stayed away from the place. I didn't visit anyone there and I would even look away when I saw a sign for it. It was as though once I recognised my own pain was sourced there, or felt like it was, I treated the town like something that could really harm me and wanted to avoid it. So, when I knew I had to go to see my sister and be with my family, I called Joe, and he left work and came to meet me without hesitation, going with me when I drove up there.

On the way I realised this was the first time he was going to meet my family. Talk about a baptism of fire, meeting them in such stressful circumstances. He didn't seem fazed; he was putting me first and that made it easier.

The next time he met them was in better circumstances. With my sister out of hospital and my family in better form, we went up to Coleraine to celebrate Jamiee-Leigh's birthday. Everyone was there, so he met my whole family. What was strange, though, was that they didn't like him at all.

We moved in together anyway.

20

Witness for the Crown

Telling my father was really difficult.

'It's going to court soon, so I thought you'd need to know before you see it in the papers,' I emailed him.

I pressed send and went to make a cup of tea, and before the kettle had boiled my phone rang. My dad was on the other end of the line and his voice shook as he said my name. He had, I suppose, just got the worst news of his life.

'I'm so sorry, pet,' he said, 'I should have been there.'

I knew he meant that, and I knew he felt that, but he and my mum were kids themselves when they had us. It's just not reasonable to expect huge maturity out of teenagers, no matter if they're married or not.

I do think, though, that if my dad had been more involved, he might have asked me something that sparked a confession from me. I used to dream about that sometimes when I got older, that my dad had asked me if I liked Davy, or if anyone was hurting me, or something. In my daydreams I would admit the abuse and watch as my dad beat Davy to a pulp. It used to keep me going, that daydream.

I have no doubt that my dad felt the guilt he was expressing to me over the phone. I see no reason to smooth over the impact on children when men abandon families, but it doesn't mean my father was a bad person. However, there were consequences to having an absent father. If he had been involved with us, would Davy have felt confident enough to abuse me?

When I was little, I missed my dad a lot. I used to wish he was in Belfast, not far away in England. I used to ask him on the phone when he was coming back. I think back then, and sometimes even now, people think their actions have no consequences for their children, but they do.

When I was a little girl I used to dream that my father was the man in my house and that Davy was a stranger I never knew. As an adult I often wondered who I would be if my father had not had an affair and left my mum, or even if he had not left Belfast. Sometimes I look in the mirror and wonder who she is, that untouched and unharmed woman who grew up with innocence and calm.

'Let me know when the case is,' my dad said. 'I'll be wanting to know how it's going.'

'I will, Dad, thanks,' I said.

I had a new job, in the local government offices, applied for on a whim as it was closer to where I lived. I was glad to be out of the bank. The posters and sponsorships for rugby were hard to see.

Gemma and I were seeing more of each other because my sister Catherine – her best friend – was in England at university. The age gap did me the world of good – people my age were settled, but the excitement and fun I shared with her was a tonic to my depression. It kept me going, meeting up and going to bars. We did silly things, like going to Build-A-Bear and getting one made up.

Two grown women giggling over outfits on bears and buying little beating hearts to put inside.

'I'm getting this one,' Gemma said, holding up a white Hello Kitty and showing me.

'Perfect,' I said and chose one for myself too. We were, I think, reclaiming a childhood that was stolen from us. I had been in toy shops before, don't get me wrong, but there is no joy in toys and fun like that when the person holding your hand is the one you're afraid of.

One day around that time, a couple of months after I told my dad what had happened to me, I got a letter. From the brown envelope, closed with a small piece of tape and with a crinkly window showing through to my name and address in plain font, I knew what it was.

'You are invited to be a witness for the Crown Prosecution.'

A witness? My body went hot and I couldn't swallow. I was not a witness; I was a victim. The word worried me. Witnesses were hammered, battered, proved liars. That was ahead of me, there was no way to stop it. I had to face it now.

I called the policeman who had interviewed me. His name was Adam Boyd, the same name as my maternal grandfather. 'Do I need a solicitor?' I said.

'You'll have our legal team,' he replied, 'they'll be in court with us, you are part of our prosecution, so the barristers and the solicitors are working with you, on our team.'

'Do I have to meet with them?' I asked.

'On the day, we will all meet together,' he said.

I cannot express how it feels to be living in the days leading up to a court case like that. I cannot even find words to cover the physical sensations of the anxiety of it, but I felt like my skin was a huge electronics board and sparks would go off in lines across it, across my cheek or shoulder, and then run into my hands and to the tips of my fingers. I would rub my hands together, but that made it worse. My muscles were on high alert, like I needed to be ready to scratch and claw and fight. My back ached, my stomach turned constantly like a boiling kettle in my belly, hot and tumbling. I felt dizzy, sweaty and unsafe, even in my bed in a locked room. I kept bursting into tears, at work, on the bus. Finding huge sobs erupting from my throat before I even realised. I would clutch at my heart, unable to fill my lungs, stretching my neck in an attempt to gulp the air. A fish out of water.

I had to explain in work what was going on. There are only so many 'I'm fine's a boss will accept when she finds her employee staring into space or with red eyes.

'You take as much time as you need, when you need it,' I was told, but I kept on trying to function. I knew if I stayed at home, I wouldn't open the curtains and I would be back to square one. I just needed to get to the eighth of October.

Then one day, on my way to work, I got a call to say that the court date had been postponed.

'For now, there is no date,' the policeman on the other end of the line said. 'The judge had to leave the case, and a new one needs to be appointed ... It's not a swift process.'

I felt like I had been punched in the gut. I was up against the wall and my anxiety spiked.

'Amanda, I'm so sorry,' he said.

I said I'd call him back, I had to get off the bus. It had turned into a furnace and I couldn't breathe at all.

I found myself standing at a bus stop I didn't know, my hands on my knees, doubled over and gasping for a breath. There were searing, racking pains in my chest. I fully thought I would pass out, my head went so light, and there was a moment when I almost fell over.

It passed – it felt like it would never end, but it did.

I called my boss, sniffling down the phone to say I was in town and that I had had to get off the bus. 'They've cancelled the court case,' I explained.

'Where are you? I'll get someone to come get you,' my boss said.

'I have to go home,' I said, 'I need to go home.'

I crossed the road and took the return bus.

By the time I got back home I was breathing better and feeling okay, but my instinct was to bring a blanket to the couch and put on the telly, filling the room with daily chat shows and rubbish to keep my mind on something other than the utter despair I was feeling now that I had no date to focus on. The court case became a notion again, not a reality.

Stress fractures started to creep in to what had been, in my eyes, a good relationship. I think that much support being needed in what should be the honeymoon period is a real weight, and un-conditional support is something that comes from long-term love and we didn't have that. I think what we had was excitement and newness and an attraction. I think that Joe had the intention of being there for me, but the reality of what that would entail was too much. In limbo like that, finding me so stressed and vacant ex-cept for thoughts of my own trouble, my new boyfriend struggled.

On top of that my family, even after a few meet ups, still didn't like him. His sense of humour wasn't theirs, and jokes fell flat or caused upset.

I got a new date for the start of the court case, and it was in a month.

When I told Joe, he stood there thinking, pressing his hands together and looking at the floor.

'Maybe you could go stay in Ballymoney when it's on,' he said.

I went into appeasement mode. 'Yes, sure that makes sense,' I said, even though it didn't make sense.

'It's not that I don't want to support you,' he said. 'I just don't think I'm good at it, I don't think I'm the one who should do it.'

I didn't say anything.

'The way you were last month, when they called it off,' he said, 'I'm not able for that.'

'No, I get it,' I said. 'It would be too much … I'm too much …'

'You're not too much,' he said, but we both knew I was. 'I'm just not going to be able to be here for you, for support … not in the way you need. I think you're better off in Ballymoney.'

I nodded along, of course – no problem, you're right. I wanted to stay at home, but putting up a fight was something I was not emotionally able to do. I had been raised in a house where the man called the shots or we faced violence, I was conditioned to lay low, I was structured that way. My survival instinct was to go quietly. So even though it frightened me, even though I wanted to be at home, I agreed. I would go to stay in Ballymoney for the duration of the court case.

I was going to face the lion while staying in the lion's den.

On the night before the first day of court, as I was packing to go and stay in my mother's house after the trial began, flowers arrived from my father. I'd never had flowers delivered before and it really touched me to receive them. A huge bouquet of roses and chrysanthemums, with baby's breath and crinkly plastic wrapped around them with a bow, and a card that said, 'We are so proud of you, love Dad and Deb'. I took a moment with those flowers, smelling them over and over and holding them against my heart. I arranged them in a vase and set them on my sideboard, then I continued sorting my things out and cleaned the house before my mum came for me. When she arrived, Joe was in his den playing computer games. I popped my head in to say goodbye. He barely lifted his head and I left.

21

Going to Court

There was no need for an alarm, but I had set one anyway. I hadn't slept at all, the increasing pressure of the knot in my stomach that had been building for weeks was at its peak. I had a lump in my throat, the kind that makes you feel like you might scream out. Perhaps that is the best way to shift it, but I swallowed it down.

'My voice is going already,' I said to my mum as she passed me in a cup of tea and a bit of toast with butter scraped across the top.

'I know you won't want to eat that,' she said, 'but give it a go, you'll need something.'

I looked at her and nodded. We were helpless; two prisoners on our way to the gallows.

I stared at the toast and nibbled the edge of it, but it made me feel sick, so I simply held it in my hand as I sipped the tea.

I got into the shower and, as I stood under the water, everything felt surreal and I wondered if I would be sick. I got out, dressed myself, brushed my hair and put make-up on like I would on any day. For court I had picked out a black suit with a red top and black heels. If I was a mess on the inside, nobody would know – I was determined to look well, but I was also cautious not to wear too much make-up. I had seen firsthand the way the courts and the media treat women based on how they dress. I wore my hair in a ponytail and prepared myself as though I was going for an interview. That way I hoped I would look 'right' for the people who were ready to tear me apart.

I wished I was going for a job interview.

In my jacket pocket I placed a stone that I thought of as my lucky charm. It was an old Irish style worry stone, smooth pieces of polished stone with an imprint for your thumb. The tradition goes that you rub your worries into the stone.

When I came back into the living room my two sisters were sitting on the sofa.

'Good morning!' I said with a sarcastic air. Catherine stared at the floor and Lorraine looked at me with wide eyes – we could feel each other's nerves, the air was static with them.

'Are we ready?' my mum asked us.

'Not really,' I said and sat down for a minute. 'I'm dressed but I am not ready.'

'Have you what you need to bring?' my mum said to my sisters, and then set her eyes on me for my answer. I nodded.

I looked at Lorraine, then at Catherine. 'Right,' I said, 'will we do this?'

'I suppose,' Lorraine said, and we all stood up.

It was a green mile to the car, a march to the gallows. My stomach churned and I ran over possible answers to the barristers over and over in my head.

I heard the words, *You're nothing but a liar, aren't you?* Over and over. Is that what they would say to me? How could I speak clearly enough that they would believe me? What could I do but tell the truth?

It took forty minutes to get to the car park of the courts in Antrim. We played music the whole way there and talked about silly things, funny memories of growing up, pointing out the window on the way, reminding each other of times we had had.

'Remember we done that photo in Tunisia and that man walked by and photobombed us?' I said.

'Oh, Jesus, I do,' Catherine said. 'Sure we had piled the drinks into us before.'

'We are a good family,' my mum said, 'all of you have fierce loyalty. It's great to see.'

'We could be tearing each other's heads off but if anyone even so much as looks ...' Catherine said and Lorraine finished off, '... we would turn on them together!'

'It's true,' my mum said.

'I am glad I'm in this family,' I said. 'It would be a lot worse to face this on my own.'

My mum turned into the car park. 'This is it,' she said.

'Oh, Jesus, I feel sick.' Lorraine spoke for everyone in the car.

My hands were sore and I rubbed them against each other as we exited the car and walked towards the main door of the court. I was on my guard, my eyes darting left and right, scared of spotting Davy on his way in.

Through security and into the main building of the court, I didn't see the police liaison officer immediately, so I went up to the reception desk and they told me there that we should wait on one of the benches and someone would come for us soon.

It's hard to describe how I felt sitting on that bench with my mum and sisters. The wait felt like it went on and on, each one of us watching the door for Davy. Terror was emanating from my mother as she sat beside me, picking at the threads in her coat over and over until she lifted them, and her breath was coming in spurts. She was pale and I could see tiny veins in the skin around her eyes, damage from years of beatings. My sister Lorraine was rubbing her hands back and forth on her thighs as if she was trying to warm them. Catherine held my hand, the sweat from both of us cold and clammy, but we didn't let go.

A woman came over to us then. 'Amanda?' she said to Lorraine and Lorraine pointed to me. I stood up, fast. I wanted her to take us somewhere else, anywhere else. We couldn't stay there, it was terrifying.

'I'm Karen, from witness support, and this is Martin.' She pointed at a man who was a few steps behind her, looking apologetic.

'Hello, hello,' he said to each of us, taking our hands in a weak handshake. 'Come with us, upstairs, come this way,' he said.

Thank God. We were getting out of the throughway, away from the traffic, away from Davy.

Upstairs there was a little seating area, away from the main lobby of the court, lit by a large skylight that threw bright daylight onto one side of the room where there was a large plant, a sofa and a coffee table covered in magazines.

'This is nice,' my mum said. I could see colour returning to her cheeks and she was breathing normally again, now she was out of harm's way.

'There are loos up here,' my sister Catherine informed us as she spotted them. It felt like a refuge, a safe zone. I was incredibly glad of it.

Karen offered us tea or coffee, which we accepted, settled a little bit by the isolation from the busy court, and then, while we drank, she explained to us that this little area was ours to use each day and we could just come and go how we pleased from there.

'It's out of bounds for members of the public,' she explained, giving us reassurance, 'but there might be other families, other victims, up here sometimes.'

We understood that, and Karen reassured us only victims could use the room. Nobody else could go up there.

'You can bring food and use the fridge,' she said. 'Maybe you won't want to use the canteen – it's open to everyone, the public and ... the defendant.'

She stood up and showed us a door. 'The court is through here, you can go in and out using this door.'

'Where is David Tweed during the case?' Lorraine asked. She blurted it out as though she had been holding the question in during the rest of the tour.

Karen sat back down and looked solemn. 'Mr Tweed will be in the communal area, or in one of the rooms if his team have secured one.'

She reached over with her two hands and patted my two hands where they were holding onto my knee.

'If you need to check who is out in the public space there, if you need to go out there, I will check,' she said, with a very serious face. Her tone comforted me; she knew this was not easy.

I felt better having Karen.

The entrance to the space darkened with the unmistakable shape of a barrister, grey wig plopped on top of his grey hair, a high white collar closed with a black pin tight around his neck, and a black cloak falling off one shoulder. He arrived with Adam

Boyd, the policeman who had originally interviewed us, who gave us a nod.

'Now!' The barrister said with a big smile. 'Who have we?'

'I'm Amanda,' I said and he repeated my name loudly back at me, shaking my hand with gusto.

He did the same with my sisters and my mum.

'My name is Rick Weir,' and he sat down on top of some magazines, rose again to remove them and sat again. 'How are we all holding up?'

In unison, we all replied that we were okay.

'I'll be glad when it's all over,' I said and Rick nodded with his eyes shut and pressed his mouth closed firmly in sympathy.

'Very difficult, very difficult,' he said.

'It is,' my mum said.

'Lorraine, Amanda,' he said, 'could we take a minute for a chat?'

There were rooms off that lobby area and we followed Rick into one, where there was a table and chairs and a television on the wall with a camera. Rick sat on the other side of the table, with the solicitor and the police victim support worker.

'This is the room for video link, for evidence,' Rick explained as he saw us looking at the camera. 'If you prefer to give evidence here, you may. I feel it's stronger for the jury to see you in person, in front of them, rather than on a screen, but it is up to you, ultimately.'

'I want to stand in the court,' Lorraine said.

I looked at her. I did too.

'Have you seen a trial before?' he asked.

We shook our heads as neither of us had.

'What you see on the television … it won't be like that. There'll be no shouting or slamming of hands, and at times it might seem as though it is going around in circles, but I promise you everything we are doing is pushing to secure a guilty verdict.'

He told us that Davy would be in the court, behind a screen, for the entire proceeding. Then he said we would stand facing the jury and the judge. 'You will be able to see Mr Tweed and the court,' he said.

The solicitor then said, 'Our job is to prove guilt, beyond a reasonable doubt. It's the hard job – the defence only need to find one small doubt in our case and pass that to the jury and their job is done.'

I was focusing so hard on their words that I could barely understand them. I felt this responsibility to myself, to my younger self, to take this really seriously, and I was putting myself under severe pressure, looking back now.

Rick noticed. 'Unfortunately … cases like these, Amanda, are difficult to prove and I do need to make sure you understand that a guilty verdict will not be easy to get.'

I said nothing. I let his words rest in my mind. I was hurt by that, but I knew it was what it was.

'Just remember this, when you are out there,' Rick said, 'the truth is easy.'

When he said that I felt my resolve strengthen and my head cleared completely. The pressure that had formed around my eyes when I woke that morning lifted.

The truth is easy. Rick had no idea the impact of those words on me that morning, and to this day.

'I know court is scary, and that you are nervous. This is the last piece of the puzzle for you all,' Rick said before he left, 'but you are all very brave and no matter what the outcome of this trial, you should be proud of yourselves.'

'Thank you,' I said.

Back in the family room, I saw that people from our family had come to the court to support us all. I needed a minute, so I sat down, slightly shielded by a plant, for a moment.

My sisters were sitting, both of them, staring at the floor. Uncle Danny was standing talking to my mum. His wife was flicking through magazines but clearly reading nothing. Gemma was standing in the corner – she had lost so much weight. She was looking at me. I smiled at her and shook my head a little in the universal gesture of 'What are we doing here?' She smiled back and shrugged.

The room seemed so full of emotion, and I was still taking in the words said to me in the video room. I waited for everything Rick had said, and everything the solicitor had said, to settle, and then I joined everyone. I suppose, like any scared animal, I was hiding. The enthusiasm of the support we had, it felt like a lot. It was strong and forceful, and I could feel it without anyone saying a word, but at times it was suffocating.

Waiting for the call, it felt like the longest day of my life. I could feel every inch of my skin and my eyes felt strained. Karen was explaining to me constantly what was happening through the door – there was a legal argument being made, the jury was chosen, the judge was discussing things. Each time she came back and forth she was relaxed, catching my eye and giving me a quick smile, leaning in and touching my arm with the update.

'The barristers are just arguing a point now,' she said, and then, 'they have selected the jury now,' and on and on like that.

Then I noticed her demeanour change and she paused at the door for a minute. Then she crossed the floor and said, 'Amanda, the judge has called you up now,' and she reached out and took my hand. Even though I had been waiting for this, I started to shake violently and I felt like I needed to be sick.

Karen patted my hand as she held it, bending over to me as I sat trying to ready myself.

'You'll be alright,' she said. 'I'll be in there too, with you the whole time. I'll be right at the door, just look for me there, I'll be there.'

It was a comfort. I held myself together even though there were tears already falling down my cheeks in lines, a steady stream. I dabbed at them with the back of my hand. I stood up and brushed my jacket off and smoothed my hair back to where it was held in a ponytail. 'Right,' I said.

'Ready?' Karen said.

I laughed, nervously. 'No, but will I ever be?'

She squeezed me in a half hug. 'Let's go.'

She held me like that all the way across the room. I caught Lorraine's eye and didn't drop it until I went through the doors. I crossed the lobby to the doors of the court and went in, and then I saw him, sitting there with his head down, and I was so angry with Davy Tweed.

As I sat down, I wanted to stand back up and scream at him. I wanted to shout, 'Fuck You!' across the room. Even now, at his lowest point, held up as a child rapist in front of the entire country where he grew up and worked and had friends, he didn't care. He just wanted to control me, he wanted to manipulate and gaslight. The man was insane.

My heartbeat was booming in my chest. My mouth was dry. I took slow deep breaths and held Karen's hand. I tried to stop my knee jiggling against the bench by pushing my feet into the floor, but that made things worse. Karen squeezed my arm again. 'You're doing great,' she said and gave me a little thumbs up.

'Can we call witness Amanda Brown to the stand?' said the court officer.

22

The Interrogation

Although I was sitting there waiting to be called, it made me jump to hear my name. I got to my feet, letting go of Karen's hand as I did, and stepped out into the aisle of the court alone. The press were seated to the left of the court, notebooks and pens in their hands, and the jury was in front of me. I tried to read their faces, the ten women and two men sitting in two rows. I wondered if they were trustworthy, I wondered what their politics were, and it crossed my mind whether it was possible that Davy could know them or have warned them. I looked at the two men – were they rugby fans?

On the right as I went up were the defence team. They were closed in together, whispering and writing things on yellow pads. I caught the eye of the barrister, he seemed to look through me. The crown barrister Rick smiled, nodded and gestured for me to continue on up into the box, but I wasn't reassured by his presence. I felt like I might pass out, and my heart was so loud that I was surprised people weren't able to hear it. I sat in the witness stand, took a drink of water and exhaled. I realised I had been holding my breath.

Our barrister went over my statement. I hadn't seen it since the day I had signed it at the police station. Rick asked me about the night of the car crash.

'You say it happened on a Sunday?' he said. 'How can you be sure of that?'

I answered that I knew because I had a maths test the next day.

'And what would that mean?' Rick's tone was gentle and encouraging.

I told the truth. 'I'd studied for it, and that was rare. It's silly, but I was disappointed to miss it, and that's the only time I've ever felt that.'

'And do you have the date of this incident?'

'No,' I said, 'but if you give me a calendar I could work it out.'

'How could you do that?' he asked.

'Well,' I said, 'Children in Need was on' – I remembered the association I had made with Pudsey the bear on the night when I saw my bandaged head just like his – 'and it was just after Aunt Sharon's birthday.'

The questions went on like that, as we worked through my statement line by line.

The judge sat higher than everyone, in a wide box, with a somewhat shabby-looking grey wig on his head. He said, 'Has the prosecution any more questions for this witness?' and looked down at Rick over his glasses.

'We do not, my lord,' Rick said and sat down with the prosecution team.

'We shall take a small break now,' the judge said to everyone, his eyes landing on me as he looked around. He nodded and said I could go.

I was relieved to get down from the stand, but also conflicted, as I wanted things over with. How could I possibly eat lunch with the defence questioning session still ahead of me? I knew they would not be asking me questions with the same gentle tone and sympathy that Rick had. I knew they would be wanting to show me up, to trip me up, to give that jury just one small doubt that would see Davy announced an 'innocent man' again at the end of it.

'You did so well,' Karen said as I came back to her and she took me through the doors to the victims' area, 'you really came across so well.'

I sat with Lorraine and waited for the call back, but it never came. After about an hour Karen came in and told us the court was done for the day, at least she thought so, so she would make sure and come back to tell us either way. I was confused. The judge had said we would take a break and I was psyched up to be cross-examined.

'It's over?' I asked.

'For today it is,' Karen nodded, fully understanding the stress of it all.

'And is Davy Tweed going home too?' I said then, suddenly realising that my worst enemy was only down the road from where I was staying. I wanted to go home to my own house. I wanted my own sofa, my own bed. But Joe hadn't texted or called to see how things were going, so I just got into my mum's car and went back to Ballymoney.

'You say your memories have never left you?' the defence barrister asked. I was standing my ground. I was not going to be pushed over now.

'No, they have not,' I said, truthfully.

He walked back to his desk and checked his notes, 'And yet, Miss Brown, you were speaking to the police in 2007 and you never mentioned this abuse? Surely that, of all times, would have been opportune?'

'I didn't feel safe to do that,' I said.

I held my worry stone in the palm of my hand, my thumb pressed into the indentation. I reminded myself over and over of what Rick had said – the truth is easy. I flattened my emotions out with that reality, I was not trying to spin anything or manipulate anyone. I was telling the truth, so my part here, in this court, was easy.

'You didn't feel safe? In a police station?'

'At that time I wasn't ready, emotionally, in my life to talk about it,' I said. 'It's not the easiest thing to talk about sexual abuse.'

That morning, when we got in, people asked me if I had seen the newspaper headlines laid out in garages and newsstands all over Belfast: Former Ireland Rugby Player Davy Tweed on Trial for Child Abuse.

My uncle bought *The Telegraph*. We sat on the benches in the family area and I leaned my head on Mum's shoulder as she opened to the middle pages where our trial was covered by the paper in flashy text boxes, with photos of Davy now and back in his rugby days.

Now everyone knew. All my darkest secrets, the ones I had locked away since childhood, were out. My name wasn't there, but I felt as though it was. I felt as though I was as exposed as could be. Pandora's box was open and all the pain and evil of my story were swirling around above me, and it couldn't be closed on them ever again.

There is real despair in that realisation, especially for the abused. It's such a huge thing to admit, to come forward with, but I don't think you ever really understand the magnitude of telling your story until you read it back in the newspaper, knowing that everyone who ever knew you, people you don't like, people you do like, every person, can read about that private and sensitive thing you tried to stash away. You realise you've changed now, not only in yourself but for all of those people. You're not just you now, you're the abused person, the victim, the damaged.

I couldn't get my head around the idea that I was described as a 'witness' and not 'the victim'. I didn't understand that at all. A witness was a bystander, a person who looked on while a crime was committed. Someone who could give evidence to say what did happen. I was the victim – what happened, it happened to me. It all felt as though the wording in the paper was framing the case carefully just in case it ended up like the last one, with an 'innocent' man walking free.

I remember the way my body reacted to seeing my trauma described in the pages of the paper that day – it felt like I was being assaulted all over again. I was horrified and humiliated. For a minute I wanted to go back, but the adult I was now, Amanda Brown, took a deep breath and got on with it. The tools I had learned as a kid – how to avoid conflict, how to keep myself safe from exposure – I used them now. I showed no emotion and swallowed the fear, the anxiety and deep sadness I was feeling.

That morning the court was delayed for hours as the barristers discussed the newspapers and how that might affect the trial. We sat waiting in the halls.

The next few days were spent waiting to be called, and then being lashed at on the stand. I would have taken a physical beating any day over that verbal lashing – the latter cut much deeper. The barrister spoke to me as though I were the criminal and, although intellectually I understood that he was trying to get his client off and trying to make my evidence look doubtful, it felt like bullying. It felt like real abuse as he battered me over and over, looking for details and information that a seven-year-old would never remember – times and dates; details of ordinary things that I would not have noticed because I was being abused; every time I thought my life and my mum's life were in danger.

That's what Davy had always told me. If I didn't do what he told me, he would kill me and my mum, or throw us onto the streets.

'Miss Brown,' the barrister pressed me with the casual arrogance of a man who thinks he knows something, the type of twisted mouth that told the room he thought he was about to catch me out, 'would you admit that you could have been dreaming?'

'No,' I said. I could see Davy out of the corner of my eye. He was shifting in his seat.

'I mean it was the middle of the night ... you *could* have been, would you not agree?'

'Absolutely not, I was fully awake,' I said.

He raised his eyebrows. 'Hmmm, do you think you can be sure?'

'Yes.'

He asked me questions with his back to me, addressing them

to the court. 'Did you often wake at night,' he said, 'to use the bathroom?'

'Yes, I did,' I said.

'But Miss Brown, would you not say that you would have been half asleep when you used the bathroom?'

'Probably if it was a short run, and I would be able to go back to sleep.' I told the truth.

'Ah,' the barrister said, and he wagged a finger, 'so you could have been dreaming this happened to you?'

'That's not what I'm saying at all,' I said. 'Stop trying to put words in my mouth.'

The judge interrupted us, 'Miss Brown, you will do well to answer the questions as they are put to you.'

The barrister changed tack.

'You were married?'

'I was,' the question surprised me. I hadn't expected my current life to be quizzed at all.

'But this marriage failed? Is that right?'

'We were not compatible in the end,' I said.

'Do you blame Davy for that?' He asked.

'I haven't considered who is to blame,' I said, 'not like that, but I do blame the sexual abuse I was a victim of at the hands of Davy Tweed for the periods of depression I suffer.'

The barrister was awful. I suppose these men have to believe their client is innocent in order to defend them, but the way he questioned me was wounding. Each night of the trial I would lie awake running his questions over and over, asking myself if he was right to ask them, asking myself if I was really worth such contempt.

'And what time was that?' he had asked.

'I have no idea,' I said.

'Oh, come on Miss Brown, you are telling the court you were being sexually assaulted and yet you don't remember the exact time on the clock?'

'That's right, I don't remember,' I said.

I could see how much he despised me in his questions, how cruel I was in his mind to do this to a man. My tears balled up in my throat. I quashed them, I swallowed them.

He asked me again and again about the first assault.

'Well, you don't remember what was on the television on this night?' he asked again. 'You have … no idea?'

'Porn,' I said, 'but no, I don't remember the details of it.'

'You don't remember the details of the event?' he frowned as if confused.

I felt trapped in this cat-and-mouse conversation, where what I said was being spun into something I didn't mean, where what I knew was being called into question in the most strange and foreign way, where this professional man was trying to lure me into stumbling over my story.

I remembered what Rick had said to me. The truth is easy.

After my evidence was done, each time, I went to the ladies' toilets to let that ball of tears out. I sat on the toilet and cried my eyes out, into my hands, as quietly as I could. Then I fixed my make-up, brushed my hair and went back out for the next round.

I had no appetite, but I remember forcing myself to eat the biscuits given to us with tea in that family room in the courthouse because I would feel faint from the lack of sugar in the mornings. And I was exhausted. When we would get into my mother's house in Ballymoney each evening, I would actually fall asleep the minute I lay down. Emotional exhaustion can be more severe than physical. Sometimes I'd wake up later, uncomfortable, and find myself still fully dressed with my shoes on, and have to get up to get undressed before climbing back into the bed and trying to sleep again. But a lot of the time, once I woke I would start to run over things from the day before or try to imagine what would be ahead of me later that morning and my mind would race. My thoughts were fast and muddled. By the time the morning came I would be exhausted again, as though I had been doing hard labour. I had aching bones and an aching head.

I was first up in the court.

'So, Miss Brown, you say you told your brother, Mr Aaron Tweed, about the abuse?'

'I did, yes,' I replied with a firm nod.

'And you went to the police?'

'Yes,' I said. *The truth is easy.*

'But you didn't make a statement?' The defence was leading me somewhere, but I decided I wasn't going to try to see where this was going. I was just going to answer each question with the truth. My brain was tired enough.

'I didn't make a statement that time,' I said. 'I don't know what records the police made, or if they even did; it was just a conversation.'

'We have no record of this conversation.' The defence turned to deliver this line to the jury, as if it was some sort of gotcha.

My barrister stood up. 'My lord may I approach the bench?'

I watched the two barristers whispering in argument to the

judge, and then the judge said the court would be adjourned to determine if the police had or had not taken a record.

We all went home. It seemed so pointless. We had been there less than an hour.

23

The Truth is Easy

Four days into the trial I was ... fed up. That's the only way to describe it. My body ached, I had a constant headache, and I can say that I felt really bullied. The questions I was being asked by the defence were the same ones, over and over and over. I kept my head and spoke the truth, so my answers were also the same ones, over and over and over. My barrister was encouraging, catching my eye and giving me a reassuring nod during the battering ram that was my cross-examination. I never turned my head Davy's way, so I never looked at my support network who sat in court, as they were beside him. Rick was my only comfort and he was a good one. The press were frantically scribbling and at times I would hear my own answer and imagine a headline.

The defence barrister was getting agitated. I can understand that now, knowing that he knew he was on a losing streak. Each time I answered truthfully, the jury would feel my words were the truth, and so I know he was seeing really good evidence appear for the prosecution as he went on and on, battering and twisting, trying to throw me, trying desperately to hear me slip up or trip up. But that never happened, and I know why. Because the truth is easy.

'You've said your memory isn't clear, Miss Brown?' he asked. The jury had been handed copies of the journalling I had done where I detailed my abuse over the years.

'I wrote memories down, as they came back,' I said.

'I don't think these are your memories at all,' the defence barrister said. 'I think after Davy was accused three years ago, that someone else was constantly insinuating that you had been abused.'

'I don't know what you mean.' I was baffled.

'Why are you really saying these things about Mr Tweed?' he said.

I shook my head hard. 'I'm still terrified of him. This was about me taking a step forward.'

'And yet, you don't remember the details of the incidents you claim happened to you?'

'I'm not a robot, I'm scared, I can't sleep at night.' Why was he saying all this?

'Did your mother ask you to accuse David Tweed?'

'What?' The question came out of left field.

'As a revenge for the beatings he gave her? Did she ask you to do this? Miss Brown, can you admit your mother would be angry about the violence she experienced in her life?'

'I'm sure she is, I certainly am,' I said.

'I think this campaign against Mr Davy Tweed is one of revenge,' the defence barrister said. 'Your mother wants to do him down, doesn't she?'

'I think my mother has enough of her own evidence to … "do him down", if that's what she wanted,' I said. 'She has years of police reports and doctors' reports herself.'

I then said firmly, 'Davy Tweed abused me as a child, and as a teenager, that's the truth.' I sat up straight and looked at the jury. 'As I said, my mother has enough evidence of her own without the pain of watching her daughters talk about the abuse they suffered here!'

At that moment I saw it in his eyes, he believed me. I knew it by how his face changed, his eyes went from mocking disdain to a sort of relief, and a fury with his client. He snapped his head over his shoulder to look at his client. He knew I was telling the truth and Davy was lying – at least, that's what it felt like, that's what it looked like.

'Isn't it true Miss Brown, that your mother asked you to say these things as revenge for what David Tweed did to her?' The barrister's smirk really got to me, but I kept my cool.

'Why would my mother do that?' I asked the barrister. 'Answer me that, why would she put us all through this living hell?'

The court fell deathly quiet. It was as if realisation dawned on everyone. I saw Rick sit back in his chair with quiet satisfaction. The defence had run into a wall.

The judge spoke to me.

'Miss Brown, the witness is not who asks the questions.'

I nodded.

An argument erupted between the barristers then, and they approached the bench. I got a bit lost; I wasn't sure what was happening. There seemed to be some issue with the use of Davy Tweed's previous bad character.

'This court is adjourned,' the judge said and the entire room seemed to stand up at once with a loud clatter as he left.

Karen met me as I came off the stand. 'You must need a cup of tea,' she said. 'The way you handled that was impressive, Amanda. I would have gone under the pressure.'

'The truth is easy,' I said to her.

Back in the family room, my sister said the same.

'He was pushing you so hard, I don't know how you didn't lose it,' Lorraine said.

'He believed me Lorraine,' I said, 'I saw it in his eyes, he totally believed me.'

She shook her head gently, 'Well, it's the truth ...'

'His job is to make me out to be a liar, and he believed me.' I took the cup of tea Karen had made me and sat down. This time I didn't go to the bathroom and sob into my hands. No matter what happened now, I knew I had done the only thing I could. I had spoken my truth.

That night, back at my mum's, I saw my cousin Gemma. She called in and we had a cup of tea.

'I'll admit I'm struggling with this,' she said, 'I ...'

Her chin wobbled and she couldn't speak.

'Just stay strong,' I said. 'No matter what happens, don't let him own us, let's not let Davy fucking Tweed control us now.'

'The things he did ...' she got some words out but dropped her head into her hands and sobbed.

'I do understand,' I said. 'Let me get some tissues.'

When I came back, she had stopped crying as hard and her eyes looked huge and distraught.

'What if he gets away again?' she said. 'I don't think I could cope.' She looked down, 'I do think about escaping all of this sometimes ... I can't take my own memories sometimes ... It's like going through it all again.'

I shook my head, 'Listen to me. You are an amazing person, you have me, you have Cat, your dad, all people who are here for you. Who has he got? Nobody. Why? Because he is a monster. If anyone should kill themselves, it should be Davy Tweed.'

She looked back at me. She looked like a ghost.

When I woke up on the fifth day, the knot in my stomach was gone. The conversation I had had on the stand, the look on the defence barrister's face, it had meant the world to me. I had seen it in his face, the realisation that his client was guilty. The woman he was battering and pushing into any corner he could find was telling the truth. I wondered did he sleep that night? I hoped not.

I thought about how it would feel to think you had a client who was innocent and then realise that you were on the wrong side. I wondered was it painful, did it come with its own anxiety? Did he lie in bed the night before wondering how to go forward from there?

I had slept, replaying the moment when I saw the flinch of realisation on his face. It was a comfort. I had felt like I won. Even if things went downhill from there, I had that moment and it was good enough. I knew trials were never straightforward, especially not ones like this. I knew we could suffer a 'not guilty' verdict and have to live with that, but my moment would get me through. If that educated, honest lawyer could see the truth, others would too.

In court that morning the bad character clause had been decided. It was allowable in this trial. If David Tweed had badly battered my mother, that was going to be used as evidence that he was capable of other abuse. The defence argued that if Davy was freely admitting one part of this story – that he battered my mother – then why would he deny the other? It's always hard to wrap my head around the way the law works, it's such a complicated process, especially in Northern Ireland, but it went like that for us.

The defence didn't keep me long that morning; he just ran over some questions from the previous day once more. He was softer and less sneering and mocking in his tone. 'We conclude our questioning of this witness, my lord,' he said to the judge.

I was done. I came off the stand and for the first time I let myself glance over at Davy. He wasn't looking back, he was looking down. He was shifting in his seat and twitching. He had underestimated me. He thought he knew me. He thought he was in control of my truth, when in fact I was in control. I wanted to give him the finger. I wanted to bang on the glass and mock him. I wanted to raise both hands with my fingers in a V and give him the biggest *Fuck You*, but I didn't. I just looked away again to the doors that led from the court. I had done my best, I had told the truth and my part was done.

We went home just before lunch.

'Mum, drop me to my own house, will you?' I asked as we drove out of the car park.

My house was empty as Joe was at work. I got into the shower and put on pyjamas and got onto the couch with tea and toast, watching soaps and dramas until he got in. When he did, he gave me a big hug.

'Jesus, Amanda, I'm glad you're back home,' he said.

'I am too,' I said.

'I've survived on Coco Pops all week – I'm sick of them,'

he said. 'Make us a cuppa there will you and I'll be in on the PlayStation.' He left the room.

Over the weekend I cleaned the place and organised my clothes for the week in court to come. I knew I wouldn't be back on the stand, so I picked my outfits for comfort and ease. On the Sunday evening my mum collected me and brought me back to Ballymoney.

Lorraine was going to be on the stand that week. The realisation of that hit when I saw her sitting at our kitchen table, her lips moving as if she were answering someone, but she was not making any noise.

'You alright?' I said.

She nodded. I knew her mind was racing, bringing her through questions. She had seen what I had been put through and I knew she would be feeling the pressure of that herself now. It was all ahead of her.

'The truth is easy,' I said to her.

Lorraine is so much more of an expressive person than I am. You can tell what she is thinking just by looking into her eyes. When I said that to her and she looked up, I could see all the pain and fear and worry right there.

'You'll be alright,' I'd said. 'The barrister knows we are telling the truth now, he won't go as hard.'

Being in the court that day was, for me, so much easier. I wasn't watching the door, I wasn't running over questions in my head. I was making other people tea and checking on them.

I knew Lorraine was under severe pressure and I think I hadn't considered until then that she had had to watch everything I had gone through. She had been the one waiting for me when I was on the stand, as I was now waiting for her, but I hadn't thought about how it would feel to watch someone being tortured while knowing you were next. That would be unbearable. I knew my sister would feel huge pressure to not undo the evidence I had given, to not say the wrong thing, to not let us down.

As she was called to the courtroom, she stood and started to walk towards the door. I remember Karen's hand was out to take Lorraine's, and I remember Lorraine stretching out to take it, but her legs gave out and she collapsed. The whole room became chaotic, people attending to my sister and the court guards going to speak to the judge. Word came back that she could take a moment to recover. She was carried to a chair and sat there, while someone gave her a cup of sweet tea. As she sipped on it, tears ran silently down her face.

A constable came in, squeezing through everyone to get to Lorraine. 'The judge has said you don't need to testify, Miss Tweed, if you're not up to it?'

Lorraine shook her head. 'I'm fine now, I want to.'

After a further rest of around ten minutes, Lorraine went in and took the stand.

I don't know if you've ever seen a person getting 'triggered' in the real sense of the word. I know everyone uses that word nowadays to describe anything uncomfortable, but I saw my sister triggered in that courtroom. I saw her attempt to describe her abuse, and a look came over her that can only be described as watching her go back in time and feel the actual feelings she would have felt then. More than once she broke down in sobs that came from so deep inside they were silent and racking. I watched the barrister, unsure of what to do, and growing increasingly impatient with his 'witness', approach the bench and ask to be adjourned. The judge allowed it.

That night we all took sleeping tablets.

24

The Verdict

On the way to court the next day Lorraine was agitated.

I was sitting beside her in the car and I could feel her panicking, and I felt really angry. This was bullshit. We were being put through hell when we had done nothing wrong, nothing but be small children in the presence of a paedophile. That was our contribution to this crime – we had been in the wrong place at the wrong time, children of the wrong person, the ones that grace and God abandoned to evil. And we were not being taken care of by the justice system. We were being spoken to like we were liars, we were being questioned on our experiences, those horrific painful abuse episodes that had haunted us and tortured us our whole lives, as if we were making them up. No care was given to our mental health, nothing was done for our emotional needs. It was what it was – I get it, it's court – but I think it was wrong.

She is soft, my sister, and so the feelings she has bubble up to the surface and shape her. One of those people of whom others might say, 'she wears her heart on her sleeve' – you can see her feelings. Her father knew that about her and in the court he used it to his advantage. When I went into the courtroom to support Lorraine, I could see already that Davy was sitting there smirking, staring her way. I knew that tactic, he had tried it on me many times and succeeded in intimidating me. Because of that, from the moment the barrister started to question Lorraine, she was in tears.

'I'm sorry, judge,' she said when he leaned down to check she could continue, 'I'm sorry I'm not better at this.' He nodded and told her to carry on.

I wanted to stand up and scream, 'How could she be better at *this*?'

I wanted to roar at them and turn over tables. My sister was a victim and she was being put on trial. I wanted to leave my bench and storm up and punch through the glass protecting Davy Tweed. I wanted to smash his teeth down his throat for putting us all through lives full of misery. We lived in hell because of him. He was sitting there smirking across the courtroom at his own daughter, who he had sexually abused her whole life, and she was the one apologising.

I could feel my cheeks turning red. I felt so hot, I stood up and left the courtroom, allowing the swing door to bang wildly back and forth behind me. I went into the family room and barely got through the second door before a scream erupted out of my mouth, through my gritted teeth. With no way to express anger properly, I burst into tears.

'How dare he, how fucking dare he?' I said over and over.

The family members who were sitting in the room kept quiet as I ranted.

'That absolute bastard, how dare he look at her like that?' I said. I wanted to go back in and upend the place, drag him out from behind the screen and kill him. There he was, this big man, sitting in safety with a guard on either side while my beautiful, soft sister was being dragged over coals for information that she had guarded her whole life.

You see that's what the courts don't get. It's impossible for victims of abuse to speak with any clarity. Think about how long it takes us to admit it happened in the first place; think about how we often sit for hours in the offices of therapists and psychiatrists; how many times we opt for suicide over exposure. It's the design of the offence, it's how child molesters get away with it, by silencing their victims using intimidation. And Davy was doing it again, dismissing the distress of his own daughter, his second victim, for his own gain. I hated him. I was so angry that he put this on her, and I was so frustrated and upset too that he put it on me, but worse was the guilt I felt for not protecting my sisters. In that moment I felt real hatred, I would happily have seen him suffer. I hated him so much.

Lorraine came through the doors.

'That was okay I think,' she said, not noticing my red fury. That's the thing about me, I'm hard to read. After years of making sure that I didn't upset Davy, I can keep a straight face even when I'm murderous.

I breathed deeply and said, 'You did really well.'

'I think the defence team were quite nice to me,' she said. 'I think you were spot on yesterday, Mo. I think he knows Davy is lying.'

'I hope so,' I said, but I thought also that a person would have to be an absolute psychopath to cross-examine someone like my sister Lorraine with harshness. She breaks so openly that only the most hardened of hearts wouldn't be touched by it.

'Thank God that's over though.' Lorraine looked exhausted.

Her eyelids were swollen from the hours of crying on the stand, her nose was chafed from wiping it.

We checked with Karen to see if we were needed and, as we were not, we left the court and went home.

Lorraine had to give evidence all day the next day too, and the next.

Over that week my brother, Aaron, was also on the stand, then my poor wee mother was interrogated. She was asked about her marriage, the beatings, for evidence of Davy's bad character, and then about the disclosure by her daughter. She answered each question as it came, honestly and with her hand on her heart. I was proud of my mother as she sat up there – she is a good woman.

The following week, they called Davy to the stand.

I stayed outside. To this day I have no idea what was said to him or how he responded. Small pieces would be relayed to us, mostly by Karen, saying he was flatly denying all of it.

He was off the stand before lunch. I was raging at that. Barely a couple of hours, while myself and Lorraine were on the stand for five days and three days respectively. Nothing about this trial felt fair. I suppose that is how it feels for all victims. Perpetrators get their dues after the trial is over, we hope.

The trial went on for three weeks in total. Everything was called into question, every piece of evidence raked over and discussed. The jury was shown pages of police transcripts, witness statements and my notes. When every piece of evidence was given to them, explained and cross-examined, they went back to deliberate on the guilt of Davy Tweed.

Lorraine wasn't there for the last week of the trial. She was truly exhausted by the weeks she had put in, day in, day out in that little room in the courts. At first we thought of that room as a blessing – we wouldn't have to be out in the open of the court lobby or canteen – but soon we came to feel that, again, it was the victims who are pushed against, pushed away. Davy should have been the one in the little side room, bored of the same four walls. We should have been the ones with the freedom, but the room came to feel like something of a prison.

Sitting in that little room towards the end of the trial I wasn't expecting the verdict to fall in our favour. I had accepted what I had been told, that these trials are impossible, that juries never convict. I was satisfied that Davy had been on trial for a second time and that it would be unlikely he would be able to offend again. His charges were gross indecency and indecent assault, thirteen counts of each.

We sat in the family room, making rounds of tea, opening packet after packet of Toffee Pops and chatting about everything except where we were and what we were waiting for.

Then Karen came into the room wringing her hands and looking worried. 'The jury is back,' she said, 'they've decided on one of the counts.'

That news took us up off our seats and into the courtroom. I felt like I could not breathe. What did this mean? One count? I didn't know if they were going to decide on each count separately or if this was unusual. I hated not knowing.

The jury filed back into the spaces they had occupied for the past few weeks. I knew all of their faces so well. I'd studied them, watching for the roll of an eye or a smirk or a head shake to let me know who or what they believed. But they never gave me anything to go on.

As they sat down, I covered my mouth with my hands – I was afraid I'd be sick.

'On the first count of Indecent Assault we find the defendant not guilty,' the head juror read out.

My hands flew up to my eyes. I didn't want to know this. How could they say that?

The judge spoke. 'And have you come to a decision on any of the other charges?'

'No, we have not,' the head juror said.

The court was adjourned after that.

We were sure the jury would come back with verdicts the next day. Anything longer would be very unusual we were assured by Rick. So, the following day we went back to court and sat again in that family room. Everyone was there that day, eyes on the court door, terrified to leave for so much as a minute in case the jury would come back. We were nearing the end, on a ledge, gripping on to hope, but resolving as much as we could to let go of the idea that Davy Tweed would be convicted. He seemed too big, too enormous in the public sphere, too giant to ever be thrown down by someone as small as me.

'Teflon Tweed,' I said aloud.

Around one or so, the word came to us through a court clerk. The jury was coming back with a decision on some of the charges.

I stayed behind as the backs of my family and friends went through the doorway into the courtroom.

'I can't,' I said to Catherine as she looked over her shoulder at me and beckoned me to come.

She gestured with her hand – come.

I shook my head. I stayed where I was. The door closed behind them.

The room became suffocating. He was going to get more not guilty verdicts, I knew it. With each one I was reduced smaller and smaller to insignificance. He was getting bigger and bigger, and I was small. He was going to squash me.

I couldn't have gone into that courtroom feeling like that – I could never have allowed him to see me and know he'd won against me again. I couldn't have given him the opportunity to grin, to gloat my way. I could see his face in my mind, already gloating when I had been on the stand, the way he had looked at Lorraine.

No.

Davy Tweed loved to destroy people. He had destroyed my mother, he had destroyed Emma and the other woman, and me, and Lorraine, and Gemma. God knows who else was out there with our scars. I paced back and forth like an animal in a cage. The ball in my throat hurt and I let some tears out.

Then I heard a long scream from the courtroom.

I knew the worst had happened. Davy had won and we had lost. The status quo would remain. How could my life go on now? In that moment I felt so low, I wanted to disappear. I began to cry.

Aunt Carla burst into the room. 'He got guilty!' She wailed it and it took me a minute to understand.

'What?' The room spun.

'That dirty beast,' she said, 'they found him guilty, Amanda, he is getting what he deserves!'

I don't think I can describe the feeling of trying to take in and understand those words, having fully convinced myself that the opposite would happen. It felt like I didn't speak the language, but slowly what she said sank in, especially when the rest of my family came back to the room and their eyes were shining and their faces were bright.

'You did it!' my mum said. 'Amanda you did it! I'm so proud of you and Lorraine.'

'Seriously?' I sat down with a thump and looked up at her. 'Are you serious, Mum?'

I knew she wasn't joking, I knew this wasn't some weird prank being played on me by my whole family, but I wanted her to state it again anyway.

'Yes, Amanda,' she said, 'it's true, he got a guilty verdict.'

'I thought when I heard Carla screaming ...' I said, 'I thought he got off.'

Carla turned when she heard me say that. 'Naw,' she said, 'I was just so shocked, I'd been holding my breath!'

Uncle Danny reminded everyone there was one more verdict to come.

'So what has he been convicted of then?' I said, tensing up. Maybe the fall was yet to come.

'All counts of gross indecency and indecent assault except the one he was found not guilty of and the one left – we don't know,' he said, then hugged me. 'It's all over now, it's all over, he will definitely do time for this.'

I swallowed. The ball in my throat was gone.

I had been believed, so had Lorraine. After three weeks of punishing interrogation, we were the ones the jury believed, despite the efforts of the defence. In this situation, where the odds were so stacked against us, we had won. All the anxiety and sleepless nights of the last month were worth this vindication. It was the most challenging time of my life, but it was now one of the most worthwhile. We did what we came to do – we showed everyone who the monster was.

'Even if he isn't jailed,' I said, 'everybody knows what he is now.'

For the final verdict of the remaining charge, we all went into the courtroom. I sat in between my sisters and we held hands.

Then from behind us, a hot breath on my shoulder. I saw my sister Catherine feel it too, and we heard the whispered words, 'You lying bitches.' I knew the voice, so I didn't turn around. A female relative of Davy's was sitting behind us, it would seem. Not one of us reacted. Our lack of reaction said all we wanted to say.

The judge addressed the jury. 'Have you reached a decision on the final charge?'

'We have my lord,' the head juror said, 'we find the defendant guilty.'

There were no celebrations, just smiles of relief. After the agony of so many years of intimidation and abuse from Davy, it felt like it was over. I felt like this line had just been drawn, on the last step before the street outside the courthouse. I felt like stepping over that line was a new start for me, and everything that had gone before was left behind there. I think the others felt that way too – the life we had where Davy Tweed had power was over. This was the start of a new life, where society knew what he was and was going to punish him for it.

I wanted him to go to jail. But it wasn't up to me.

Davy blew kisses to his family as he was led away.

25

Gemma

The sentencing was set for the twenty-fifth of January. Davy was to remain in custody until then and so the city I lived in, and the town my mum lived in, took on a new freedom I hadn't known before. I felt like I could go where I wanted and do what I wanted and there was no fear. I suppose, even in areas he wouldn't frequent, I was always on edge a bit, always scared that I would pull open the door of a shop as he was coming out, or that I'd walk into a bar and see his face. Now I felt better about life; I felt like the wound that his freedom had constantly picked at could start to heal.

Then on Sunday, the thirteenth of January, just under two weeks before the sentencing, I got one of the worst phone calls of my life. I was watching television when my phone rang and my mum's name flashed up. I thought nothing of it and answered.

'Hi, Mum,' I said.

'Are you sitting down?' she said, and I could hear that her voice was high and shaky. I knew something was wrong, and I wrongly presumed it was something to do with the trial that had consumed us for the months before Christmas. I stood up and went into the hall and sat on the stairs.

'What is it?' I said.

'It's Gemma,' my mum said. 'Oh, Amanda, she killed herself.'

The hallway felt unfamiliar, my head swam, my mouth went instantly dry. I could not hear those words. Not now. Not when we were so close.

'How?' I said. 'When?'

'She hanged herself,' my mum was crying as she spoke.

'She can't have, I don't believe it,' I said. 'She can't have, we won, we beat him.'

I felt such a surge of emotions I could barely breathe.

'What about Danny?' I said. 'She wouldn't do that to him!'

My mother sounded distraught. 'He's in an awful state, I need to go. Catherine is taking it very badly and I need to go get her.'

She hung up.

I don't know how long I sat on the stairs for. I don't know what I thought, or if I had my eyes open or closed. My skin felt like it was on fire and I was unable to cry. I put my head in my hands and waited for the feeling of sadness but what I felt was anger. Deep, twisting rage in my belly. I couldn't believe it. My beautiful, funny cousin, not yet twenty-one – what had she done?

I was angry about this situation, this court case. Everything that we had focused on had taken our attention away from her and put it onto him when she was suffering so much. Now we would not have her in our lives. Uncle Danny, God help him, would have this to bear. He would never see her marry; he would never have grandchildren. We would never again celebrate her birthday, move her into her first home, watch her grow and move through the world like we wanted.

I wanted to walk out of my house and find Davy Tweed and kill him. He was the one who deserved to be lying cold in a mortuary, not our beautiful Gemma. All the healing she needed, she could have got it, she was so capable of that.

I remembered where I had been myself three years before, the times I planned to do the same. I was devastated by the thoughts I had had, the ideas that had permeated my thinking and left me so lost. I was angry at myself then. Why did I not see this coming? Of all people why did I not? I should have known it wasn't just talk, I should have realised.

I thought about the conversation we had had at my mum's table a few months before. Why did I think I was the one to deal with that level of stress in anyone? Sitting there, knowing she was gone, I thought to myself that I was the wrong person to talk to her. I was not a therapist or psychiatrist. I had so many issues myself. I had been suicidal myself. I thought I could say things that made sense to me and she would feel okay. But she had still done the worst thing.

I thought the court case was something we would all have, like a win over him. Even if he hadn't been convicted, but he *was*. Why did she do it when he had been convicted? Why did I tell her it didn't matter, why did I think words could be medicine for someone so distraught? I thought I was saying the right things, but who was I to judge? My stomach churned. I wanted to go back in time. I pressed the heels of my hands into my eyes and tried to go back.

'Just let me go back,' I whispered. This was too final. This was too much.

No matter how hard I thought or how long I sat on those stairs, the world did not pull into reverse and I was unable to change what I had been told. Gemma was dead. That was that. There was no mistake, no misunderstanding. It was what it was.

My lovely, sweet little cousin, who I had adored as a child and treasured as a woman, was going to be buried and I would never see her face again.

No.

I called my friends, the ones who knew Gemma personally and some who just knew her through me. Finally, as I heard myself say the words over and over, Gemma is dead, Gemma is dead, I started to cry.

After that, I went back into the sitting room where Joe was still watching television. He didn't look up but said, 'Was that your mum?'

'Yeah,' I said.

He still didn't look up.

'Gemma killed herself,' I said.

I went in to see her in her coffin. My aunt was sitting there staring at her daughter.

'She looks different, not herself,' she said, 'I don't know why ...'

I looked in. Mum and Catherine were there too, looking wiped out.

'It's her hair parting,' Catherine said. I was so deeply sad in that moment, realising that whoever did her hair didn't know she always wore it split to the other side. She had been tended to by strangers when here was a house full of people who loved her so much, and I hated everything about the world right then. Why was this beauty dead? What was this all for?

This house full of people, this house full of love, had scars because of Davy Tweed. Scars that would never really heal, ones that would often open and feel fresh, and that was forever. The impact of one man on an entire family who were good, it was evident in that house that day.

As everyone moved from room to room, consoling and helping each other process and cope, I stood there and wondered what would this day have been had my mother never gone to that wedding and never met Davy Tweed? What would this day have been had my dad never fallen in love with someone else and left the three of us with no home? What would it be now if I had stood up and told someone that Davy Tweed was abusing me at home at nighttime and that I needed help?

Mum took a brush and fixed Gemma's hair. Her mother smoothed her hair down with the brush and tucked it behind her cheek, and she looked like herself, as if she was sleeping. The silly Hello Kitty bear she had made that day when we were out together having fun in town was in the coffin with her. I stared at it. Her hand was still, her eyes were closed and still – she was dead.

On the day of the funeral, Joe and I drove up to Ballymoney. I took my nephew in the car with us. Minding him gave me focus and I wanted to keep it together, I didn't want to let my emotions out. I was under pressure from myself but also from a boyfriend who just didn't want or have the skills to deal with anything that had layers to it. On the drive up he tried to chat about other things, talking about holidays and other things that seemed so ridiculous to me. I felt as though I was looking out at him from this dark, black place, where Gemma was.

As we walked into the church Joe said, 'I don't know what to do with you when you're like this ...'

I felt so alone.

I sat at the back. I didn't want to lose it entirely in front of my family, and I knew I was on the edge. I got this strange idea then that grief had a hierarchy that had to be adhered to. If those closest were crying, I could cry as much as they did; if not, I could not. The service was a blur. I spent the time suppressing my feelings, pushing everything down into that familiar knot.

We drove to the graveside.

'I'll stay in the car,' Joe said. 'It's a family thing, you know?'

I nodded.

It was raining and I was so cold. They lifted the coffin to lower it and I turned my face away. I couldn't watch that, not knowing what was inside. Not knowing who was inside. How could she? *How could she?* We had come out victorious, what happened?

In the car on the way back to the house I struggled so hard not to cry. Women shouldn't put men out, right? We shouldn't ruin their mood with ours, we should never make them uncomfortable, isn't that how it goes? My boyfriend was the one who mattered, I was just an accessory. The fact that my entire world had gone dark and I was devastated, that was secondary.

While everyone was sitting around talking about Gemma and grieving as a unit, I avoided the church hall under the excuse that I was going to bring my nephew to the sweet shop. I would wait until I was alone to let it all out. I would cry when I was by myself. Because that was safe.

As we drove home that night, I physically ached from keeping my grief at bay. I wanted to howl like a wild woman, pull at my hair and bang my fists against myself. Instead, I drove looking straight ahead as the Irish countryside passed by, as Joe talked about games and friends and I made the odd sound to show that I was listening. Losing Gemma was ... *is* one of the most challenging experiences of my life to date.

When we got in, I got into the shower and sat down on the tiles with the water running over me and then I cried. I was bitter. All I kept saying was 'Why?'

But it was not why did Gemma do it?

It was a different why.

Why did I not tell on Davy Tweed years ago?

They sentenced Davy a week later. I didn't go.

I couldn't be in the building with that man for one second longer. I couldn't feel it for one more second, the way his presence made me feel. The destruction he brought to my life, it followed me like the shadow of a demon. I couldn't go there, no way. Everything was burning too wildly inside – my loss, my pain, Gemma's death, everything was too raw.

I wanted to kill him. I thought of the ways I could do it, day after day. On the day he was being sentenced I was afraid of my feelings, afraid that I would do it. He didn't deserve to breathe the air. I was also twisting with the knowledge that Davy Tweed would have heard about Gemma. I believed that he would have smiled when he heard that. His disdain for the girls he had destroyed was always so evident. He would have liked to hear that he had destroyed one of them beyond repair. It would have been the ultimate ego trip, the power he had even years later.

We had all prepared ourselves for a suspended sentence, a slap on the wrist. He deserved life.

'Four years,' my mum said down the phone to me.

'What?' I thought about that for a minute as she repeated herself.

'They gave him eight years but only to serve four,' she said.

'I don't understand that,' I said.

'It's the maximum term for those charges,' she said.

'We are being cheated,' I said.

'I know,' she said.

26

Dropped from a Height

Davy was in jail. It was a strange feeling. I had lived for so long with this fear that I would run into him, so it was new to know that I couldn't. Belfast looked brand new.

That didn't last.

Even from prison, Davy could intimidate me. Even from behind the highest four walls, with no freedom, he could control my peace. He could take it away. And he did.

'They said he is being looked after in there,' someone said.

'What does that mean? Looked after ...' I said.

'Given privileges, gone easy on,' she said, 'and I don't know but ... I suppose I should tell you that in there, people believe what he is saying ...'

'What's he saying?' I said.

'That you're lying.'

'Who is believing that?'

'The UVF.'

'Am I being threatened?' I said.

'I don't know. I don't know what they meant by telling me.'

'Jesus ...'

I became uncontrollably anxious, looking over my shoulder

again and again when I walked anywhere. I did my best to carry on with my life, to be 'normal', but the fear crept in and took over. I really started to believe that Davy was going to get me. The child who had been terrified of him was back and the woman I thought I had grown into disappeared.

Things like turning the car around if I couldn't find a space in the car park in the supermarket near the door, things like not going to the shops at all or anywhere unless Joe was with me. Things like sitting in my house waiting for a knock that never came, sure that it would and thinking that when it did, I was going to be shot on the doorstep. Things like lying in my bed listening for the breaking glass I was convinced was coming. Waiting, waiting.

I read years later that abused people will often try to cope on their own because asking for help is a vulnerability they have learned to suppress. I was like that – I still am in many ways – and so I didn't look for help with this fear. At one point I was so overwhelmed with debilitating panic episodes that I googled what I could do about them and tried all the online tips. When I felt like I was becoming overwhelmed I would ring one of my sisters to redirect my focus there, instead of on my breathing. I was so scared of what was happening to me, I was scared of my own mind, my own thinking. But I wanted to sort it out myself because I didn't trust anyone and I thought that if I went to a doctor they would put me in a mental home or slow me down with heavy drugs.

I started to use a method where I would find five things to see, four things to hear, three things to touch, two things to smell, and one thing to taste. When I found my breathing changing, overwhelmed by the unsafe world I believed I was living in, I would change direction to that small game of finding things, like 'I spy' for all my senses.

After a bad panic attack at my mum's house one time, she convinced me to go to her GP. 'Just go for me,' she said to me.

'I'm fine,' I said, but she insisted.

Thankfully, the doctor was young and holistic and asked the right questions.

'Tell me about these episodes, how often are you suffering them?'

'I get like this a fair bit,' I told him, and I explained how I was coping with the game. 'Once I get to the smelling part, I am so engrossed I feel better.'

'I think that is working for you, probably better and faster than anything I could prescribe,' he said.

Back in my mum's house I sat with my two youngest sisters, Victoria and Jamiee-Leigh. I understood why they had decided not to go to the police. Lorraine and I had done that and they had seen what we went through. It was enough for them to see him in jail for what he had done to us. They were both seeing therapists, both talking about their abuse.

I will always feel guilty that I had it in my power to say something earlier and didn't. Although intellectually I know I was a child and I was dealing with trauma in the best way I could, it really upsets me that my sisters went through it at all. I used to go over and over my memories of times I could recall Davy being around them and suddenly I would see it all so clearly and then drag myself over the coals – why didn't I see it then? Telling myself it was so obvious. The guilt became a habit and it created a heavy burden that I carried around.

Eventually, driving myself crazy with the constant whirling thoughts, I went to a therapist. I wanted to understand everything, I wanted to understand why this happened. Of course, there were no answers, that's not how therapy works. But I talked through how I felt about my dad, and how I might have felt abandoned by the most important man in my life after my parents' split. I talked about my father leaving and how that changed how I saw myself, and how Davy too, in a strange, abstract way, also left. He had arrived in my life acting like a dream dad, and so when he abused me, I lost that dream and only lived in a nightmare. My brother too had left when we were in our teens, going to England to take up a job. He didn't know how much I needed him because I never let on. My ex-husband tried to stop me when I opened up about my past, which revealed a vulnerability I wasn't able to handle. And more recently, whether it was my own guilt or any blame that was behind it, I was losing touch with the last dependable man in my life, my Uncle Danny.

I was going to England the following weekend, with a cousin and her little ones, to a town near where my father lived, and so I decided to meet my dad and ask him all the things I had ever wanted to know about the whole thing.

'Why did you leave us?' I said. 'It was like once you left Mum, you just wrote us out of your story, and that was that.'

'I suppose I thought you were happy with your mum,' he said. 'I thought it would confuse you if I popped in, you might think I was coming back ... I just thought it was the right thing. I didn't want to cause your mum more trouble than I had already.'

I gently shook my head.

'I wish I could change it,' he said.

225

'I do too,' I said.

'You're a credit to your mum,' he said, 'I'm so proud of both my kids.'

When I met my dad I could feel real love coming from him, in his words, his acts, from his eyes and expression, and it was overwhelming to realise how much I had missed out on because of how things were in the eighties and nineties and the beliefs people had about children. Back then, they believed that upsetting children was terrible, so they would hide things and pretend that things were okay and fine, not realising that children see and hear and know when things aren't right. And children make up their own answers with their immature imaginations when none are given, and usually the conclusions children come to are that things are their fault.

All that love from my dad that I felt in the coffee shop that day could have been mine as a child, if only I had spoken up and if only people had understood that children need both their parents, no matter what. That love was always there, but I had no access to it.

My past can't be changed, but I can learn from it.

Life went on.

I couldn't go anywhere near Ballymoney, I was too scared. I didn't really talk about it to anyone, I just kept my head down and stayed near my own house. I was afraid of the things I was hearing from people. Calls I was getting.

At Christmas I didn't go up to my mother's house, and I missed it terribly. I wanted the company of my family so much, but I was really scared. The road into Ballymoney became somewhere I avoided. Even the signpost startled me. Christmas since my mum had left Davy had become such a fun time, we always had such great craic even after we had all moved out, meeting back there for breakfast, coming back later for dinner on Boxing Day.

I had to suffer a constant stream of reports on Davy, how well he was getting on in jail, how many people were looking after him. I heard who was with him, who was on his side, and it scared me.

'He says he is innocent,' I heard down the phone, 'and most people believe him in there, even the prison guards are on his side and they have you branded as the liar.'

That was stomach-churning and terrifying.

Of course Davy was playing the victim. Of course he was. There was no way a man with such delusions, a man who tread the line of evil so casually and easily, no way a man like that would admit his wrongdoings. He had to keep up the appearance of a victim of women, otherwise he would need to look in the mirror and see the monster staring back at him once and for all. I knew that would never happen.

I distracted myself with work. I threw myself into my role, taking on any extra tasks and fully immersing myself in my career. I did that so well I got promoted, and it was a good distraction from any of the feelings I should have been facing; it distracted me from my memories and from connecting with my past in any way. Despite the lack of support in my relationship, I threw myself into that too, being the perfect partner, submitting to the role of the girlfriend, the woman. And I found myself engaged to be married and planning a wedding.

I threw myself into being a daughter, a sister, an aunt to my nephew and to my new niece, my sister Victoria's daughter. I took my nephew for weekends, overnights when I could. And as soon as the new baby was in need of babysitting, I took her too. I spent my spare time with the children, building Lego and watching movies. I focused on them.

But these were all distractions from another monster I was facing. The one that was eating me from the inside out.

I lived like that for as long as I can remember. Distracting myself with one event after another. In 2015 I organised a wedding, marrying Joe in an elaborate ceremony. We talked about the future and I made plan after plan in my head.

'Let's have a baby,' I suggested and then put the focus on that, falling pregnant not long afterwards. I was excited. I just wanted to forget about Davy and have good things happen, wonderful things. I could be a mother and a wife and never look back.

Pregnancy is the ultimate distraction, but it didn't work out. At the point where you're advised you can start to tell people, I lost the baby. I hadn't even had a scan yet.

Calling to cancel all of the appointments written into my diary, the obstetrics and sonogram, that was hard. But the next day I got up, got dressed and went back to work, refusing to let the world see any emotion. I could go back to the distraction of work now.

After that we couldn't get pregnant again, and so in 2016 our doctor decided we should look into IVF. That was something I could really focus on, reading all the pamphlets, going to the appointments, having tests and doing the routines as I was told. We were on the waiting list. I focused on it, looked forward to it. In the back of my mind, pushed way into the background, was the nagging thought that Davy's sentence was running out. It was four years since his sentencing, and though I was trying to ignore it, I knew that any day now he would get out. That would happen no matter what I was focusing on, no matter what I was organising. That would happen anyway.

On the twenty-fifth of October in 2016 I was on a bus going home from work, after a normal day, feeling okay, planning a night watching television, and just as I was passing the courthouse, my friend rang me.

'Jesus, Amanda, did you hear the news today?' she said. She sounded frantic.

'No,' I said, 'I'm on my way back from work, what's happened?'

'Davy Tweed's been released on appeal,' she said.

I didn't know what that meant. I knew it didn't mean that he got out early, there was something else, something in the word appeal that filled me with dread and set my teeth on edge. I knew everything was about to change.

I texted my husband, knowing he would have immediate access to the internet and the news and could text me back. I didn't want to search the words myself.

My husband sent a link to an article and I clicked it: 'Former Irish rugby international has child sex abuse convictions quashed'.

I read the first line: 'Senior judges confirmed the outcome following a hearing at the Court of Appeal in Belfast on Tuesday.'

The article continued, 'With the issue of a possible retrial still to be decided, no further details can be given for legal reasons. Tweed, 57, is set to be released from custody where he has been serving an eight-year prison sentence. The one-time elected councillor, from Clonavon Terrace in Ballymena, hugged relatives after the verdict was delivered.'

The judge had apparently said, 'There's no reason why he shouldn't be free as soon as possible.'

I felt like I was being dropped from a height. My stomach was in free fall. How could this be? What appeal? I hadn't even heard he had been granted one.

I rang my mum.

'Did you hear?' she said as soon as she heard my voice. 'I didn't want to call you until I knew you were home from work.'

'I heard just now, I'm on the bus,' I said.

'I just heard myself,' she said.

'How could they not tell us?' I said. 'Does Lorraine know yet? Where is she now?'

'At home,' my mum said. 'I'm hoping I get to tell her first.'

I said, 'Tell her now, Mum, ring her now.'

'Okay, I will,' and she hung up the phone.

I sat on the bus staring at my phone. What was I supposed to do? How had nobody told me this was happening, that this was a possibility?

I thought about my barrister, Rick, and I emailed him on the spot, asking him what was happening and saying I would appreciate some information on how Davy Tweed was able to just walk out of prison without anyone telling me.

He wrote back straight away, asked me to come to his office the following morning.

When Lorraine and I arrived the next day we were told, 'It means that the trial we had is void, because they accepted the argument that the jury in our trial was not properly briefed on the bad character clause.'

'And that's it?' I actually laughed.

'Yes,' Rick said, and I could feel his frustration bubbling beneath his formal tone.

'The judge told them when they could use the clause,' Lorraine wanted to be sure we had this right, 'but not when they couldn't?'

He nodded firmly, 'Yes.'

'And because of that he is free,' she said, 'as if there was never a trial?'

'Yes.'

'Jesus Christ,' I said, 'he was found guilty of abusing children and now that's just away, is it?'

We knew about our sisters, we knew what they'd suffered, we knew he had abused Gemma and now she was gone. I could not believe this. How could this be justice? Lorraine kept looking at me and I kept looking at her, because we knew what the other was feeling. It was such a kick in the teeth, but also we were scared. After everything we had been through, to have him 'win' like this? It wasn't fair.

'We can go for a retrial,' Rick said.

'What's that?' Lorraine asked.

'Try Davy for his crime from the start,' he said.

'The whole thing,' I said, holding my stomach, 'from the start again, the whole thing?'

'Yes, a full retrial, with a new jury,' he explained, 'but do consider the fact that Davy has spent four years in jail already, so even if we do secure a conviction, he would be unlikely to do any further jail time.'

Lorraine shook her head and I could see the idea was too much already.

'We need to think about that,' I said.

27

A Feeling of Love

'I can't,' Lorraine said as soon as we got into my mum's car. She collected us outside the barrister's office.

'Can't what?' my mum asked and I saw her grip the wheel of the car tight. She was freaked out too.

'They want to do the trial all over again, the whole thing,' I explained.

My mother's mouth dropped open. 'The whole thing?' She couldn't believe it either.

'Neither Lorraine nor me think there's much point,' I said, 'he won't go back to jail either way.'

'I can't,' Lorraine said again. 'I'm feeling so much better lately, I don't want to go through that again.'

'I feel the same,' I said. I knew I was not mentally capable. I was barely getting through this normal life I was insisting on living. I was struggling so much anyway, there was no way at all I could go backwards and sit facing that man, that monster, again. I thought about that family room, the victims' room, in the court and I felt a shudder go through me. I couldn't do it.

'We have done what we can to stop him,' I said, 'I don't think going through another trial will bring us anything but more pain.'

'We're not doing it,' Lorraine said. It was decided.

The legal system had failed us. We had been let down on a technicality and Davy was going to have that to lord over us, but we could not go through another trial, we would not survive.

Davy was free.

I encouraged my mum to renew her non-molestation order against Davy, but she wasn't able to get one because the judge decided he didn't pose a threat.

My mum was in Ballymoney, my sisters were in Ballymoney, and so was Davy Tweed. I worried myself sick. I kept imagining him at their door, late. I wondered would the neighbours turn the same blind eye they had for years as my mother got battered up and down that house? I knew they would. I begged my mum to move out of there, to come back to Belfast, but she couldn't, she said.

'Jamiee-Leigh is still in college, I can't move until she is finished, then I will,' she said.

'Have you seen much of him?' I just wanted her free of him. He had been out of prison a month.

'I keep seeing him, Amanda,' she said.

'Oh no, Mum,' I said.

'Even at the doctors,' she said, 'he was sitting there.'

'Thats horrible,' I said. I was so angry hearing that.

'Lorraine saw him down at the shops, she just left her trolley there and came home.'

'This isn't fair,' I said. I couldn't imagine how it would feel to turn a corner and have him standing there. I felt under pressure where I was, and they must have been under ten times that.

'How's things at home?' my mum asked me then and I went quiet.

'Fine,' I said.

I was lying. The night before my husband had suggested he move into the spare room for a while and I hadn't argued with him. The news of Davy's release had brought me out of my focus. I had dropped the ball. It was like we were holding hands and smiling, but suddenly I realised my hand was empty and he was standing far away. It wasn't that we drifted apart, we were pushed apart because the real me had come between us. My husband didn't want to be married to someone with such deep grief. And I could not keep up the pretence.

'I'll just sleep in there for a bit,' he said, and he did and we never talked about it again. It was over.

I thought about the babies I had planned and I grieved for them, crying into my pillow. Would this always be my life? Could I have no happiness? What had I done to deserve a life sentence, when Davy Tweed was free?

I really cried over the life I wanted and couldn't have. The babies, the loving husband, the warm and cosy home, I felt like I would never have anything close to it. The universe had other plans, but I didn't know that then.

I booked myself a holiday and when I came back I found my own place.

'We will have no peace until he's dead,' my mum was on the phone. I had gotten a letter from her solicitor and was calling her about it. Davy was accusing me of hiding money that my mother had. They were getting divorced and he was, of course, making it difficult.

He had the power to contact us again and was desperate to upset, control and manipulate us. The divorce had given him power, and he was going to use it. He never failed to stoop as low as he could to get us. It was never going to stop, he was never going to go away. This was it forever. He had ruled me as a child, harassed and abused me my whole life, and he was going to continue.

I sent letters from my bank to his solicitors and an affidavit stating I had never banked money belonging to my mother.

Just leave us alone.

I was renting a small place from a friend of mine and I was going out a little bit in Belfast with friends. My husband and I weren't speaking and as I supported my mum in her divorce, I prepared for the fact that I would go through one too, for sure. I felt so at sea with nothing to focus on, so I decided to get a mortgage and buy a house. This was something that could distract me from the depth and darkness of my own thoughts – a new direction and a place to set my eyes and future.

Getting all the finances together, saving the deposit, attending viewings and making calls gave me something to do other than be alone with my thoughts. I found a little place I liked, made an offer and it was accepted.

I went on a rare night out to celebrate, met a guy, had a few dates, and by the time I moved into my home I was five months pregnant. I had everything I had ever wanted – my own home that was warm and cosy, and a baby on the way. I was just missing the partner and that made me feel disappointed and upset, because I had decided that that was my gauge of happiness. I didn't think I could feel happy without this picture I had drawn in my mind, the kind with a white picket fence around it. I wanted that so much, but I will admit I was resigned then to it just being baby and me.

I wanted to be a mummy so much, I was tired of being told I was the best aunty, I wanted to be someone's mum. I wanted the traditional role, the baking, the playing and going on outings. I wanted to be part of that; my memories of my early life in a happy family had solidified that ideology in me. That was happiness, that was what life was about.

Being pregnant and single was hard then, because I wasn't in the picture-perfect family that I had always seen myself being part of. Being a single mother was not a dream I linked with happiness.

When my son was born, three weeks early, I had a crisis in my mind. He wrinkled his tiny forehead up and his eyes went wide as can be as he saw his mummy's face, but I felt as if I didn't recognise him, like I wasn't connecting, not in the way I thought I would. The overwhelming love I was supposed to feel was not there. I had imagined a gush into my heart, a feeling of adoration and care for the baby, but, if I'm honest, I felt a bit empty. I told myself I was just exhausted. I'd had a difficult delivery and I told myself things would change. I took him home and minded him as well as I could. I changed him, dressed him, bathed him and fed him. I totally forgot about my own needs and looked after him. I did everything I could to keep him well and calm, and I still didn't realise that *is* love.

'Maybe I should give him up,' I said to my mum, and on hearing my own words I burst out crying.

'What on earth?' She was so surprised I'd said it. 'Why would you do that?'

'He deserves a mum who can love him,' I said.

'Oh right,' she said, 'he does aye.'

I cried harder. 'I don't connect with him, it feels like I don't even care about him.'

'What are you on about?' My mum shook her head. 'See that wee boy? A wet nappy hasn't stayed on that child for so much as a minute, that's how much he is loved.'

I sniffled a bit and stopped crying.

'Love is doing, when you're a mum,' she said. 'When they can't *feel* it, you find ways to *do* it.'

I thought about my childhood and how little my mum had ever said the word love to me, how few hugs I'd had, how I'd never been called any terms of endearment. And then I thought about the clothes folded on my bed, the clean bathroom where I brushed my teeth, the warm breakfasts she made and the packed lunches and the good dinners, even on the days she was bruised and battered. I thought about that 'porridge' on the floor that Christmas, vomit expelled from her stomach with punches and kicks, and I remembered the next morning coming downstairs and seeing the disaster there. But then on the actual morning of Christmas we came down to a perfect tree decorated with baubles and tinsel and all the presents mended that had been ripped. I thought about my mother, being beaten by a giant she could not escape, smiling anyway and telling us it was okay and not to worry. I realised love looks like many things, love is doing. Love is the truth, and the truth is easy.

'What if I screw him up with my shit?' I asked her.

'He will be all right,' she said, 'he has his lovely mummy.'

The wounds of my childhood would not touch this boy, I vowed it right there. I would make sure he was untouched by the pain I had suffered. I would protect him in every way I wasn't. He would live in an open, light space and be free to be a child. This child would not be abandoned. Even though his father was not living with us, even though we didn't get on and he only saw his son a few hours a week, I knew for sure that my child would never feel that loss as I had felt mine. I would be both parents, I would fill in the blanks. I would pour such volumes of love onto this kid, he would never know the difference.

I remember when he was eight months old – I can remember the day – I was following him on my hands and knees as he learned to crawl, and he learned quickly, becoming a fast-moving object within days. This one day I was crawling after him down the hall, calling his name. He would sit back onto his bum and turn his face to me and laugh before taking off again around the house, out into the hall and into the kitchen with a squeal.

I called him as he got to the sitting room and I said, 'Where are you going?' in that sing-song voice I used only with him, and it made him laugh. So I said it again, and he laughed so hard his tiny arms couldn't hold his weight and he lay down on the rug with his face turned towards me.

I lay down with him face to face. I felt it there, a surge of emotion through me like a wave. It pushed up into my lungs and made me inhale sharply and tears stung my eyes. It was the feeling of love.

I knew it was okay, right then. I knew I was alright. I knew he had a mummy who loved him so much. I figured out in that moment that this child couldn't care less if I wasn't baking cookies and making finger paintings with him. He had no interest in a white picket fence. He just needed to know that when he looked over his shoulder I would be there behind him. I knew that was the point, that was where the love was. I would always make sure he had that.

From then on, I mothered my way, as Amanda.

Having my son made me think about the person I am, and how I had been with the men I chose up to that point. I realised that I was always trying to make something of them, to save them from mediocrity, to bring them love that I felt would make them into the man I dreamed of. I thought I could change them. But the truth was that I was choosing badly, I had settled down twice with men who didn't know what love was – they just wanted the woman in their life to be smiling and amiable. They didn't have room for reality, they were turned off by it. I wanted to be that perfect wife to both of the men I lived with, I wanted their lives to be better because I was in them, because I had learned along the way that the only value I had was through their eyes.

Now I knew that was not true. Now I knew I had value and worth all on my own, as a human.

It was as though all of that understanding opened a portal to good fortune and suddenly everything was working out. My mum and Jamiee-Leigh moved into a new home back in Belfast, and my other two sisters moved into their own homes less than five minutes from me in either direction. We were home again, creating a little community. My mum would come around to help me with my new baby, washing him, changing him, listening to me cry about all my worries and fears for him.

'I don't want to ruin his life with my shit,' I would say.

'Ah you're a great mummy,' she would reply.

Having everyone back in Belfast and near me was such a blessing. Where I had felt totally detached, now I was re-attached. My strings were strong. Lorraine's new house became a hub, because of where it was, and we all met there, going in and out, almost daily. Just as my childhood had revolved around my granny's house, our kids had Aunty Lorraine's house, where they could meet their cousins and family, and learn about life. When I went back to work, my mum minded my son, and I was so grateful for that. One place I always knew I was loved and cherished was with my maternal relatives, and I knew he would have that same experience.

The pandemic came in 2020 and like many people I was able to work from home. Just before it was announced, I got a roommate – a colleague who moved into my spare room. Thank God for him, as we went into isolation not long after and that wasn't easy with a two-year-old. I was working in customer service, but in an area that couldn't close up, so I was answering phones and emails and having meetings in my home. I used the television as a babysitter, popping my toddler in front of it while taking meetings and phone calls. I felt such guilt when he would look for me in the middle of those meetings and calls and I would have to tell him to be quiet. It was an awful environment for a baby. And unlike the workplace, there was no home time, I often found myself working late nights and through breaks because everything was so disjointed and confusing.

My mum left bags of groceries on our doorstep now and again, but we missed her so much. I didn't see anyone but my housemate and my son for weeks. I had nothing else to do but work and think, and when I would lie in my bed late at night I would think and think.

I thought about how I was now, and I would think about how I had been a few years before and I realised I was doing really well and that I was thankful to be here in this house for the lockdown. Thankful for what I had and where I was.

I thought about the years of my childhood and how it would have been if we had gone into lockdown then. I imagined that and found myself in tears, knowing that the likelihood of my mother surviving lockdown with Davy would have been slim. Already we were seeing women being killed in domestic assault cases all over the UK. I felt sure that my mum would have been murdered if she had been in lockdown with Davy. The shudders that ran through me thinking that almost lifted me from the bed. I knew that the abuse would have been worse too, if we had been locked in back then. I worried so much about all the children I knew who had no relief at that time, no school, no street to play on, no play dates, no granny's or aunty's house to get away from the person who frightened them, no relief from the terror. As an abused child I knew that you lived in terror at home and that it was only on the outside that you could let your guard down. The closer you were to home, the more unsafe you felt. It's the opposite of the childhood experience. It confuses your instinct, makes your own judgement feel unreliable. You can't trust because you don't learn trust.

The experiences of children living in lockdown in homes where they were being abused weighed heavily on my mind. So once I got the hang of working during office hours and clocking off when I should, I took an online course in mental health for children. I wanted to do something and even though I didn't know what I could do, I decided to be proactive. I wanted to understand trauma in relation to my own life and be able to apply that to others.

It was one of the best things I have ever done. One thing after another came up on the course that triggered me, and I would find myself time and time again opening small windows into my own persona. The face I showed others was moulded from my experience. My wounds opened fresh during that course and the follow-on ones I took, and I started on a healing journey. I am still on it.

People write advice so easily, often without real lived experience of their own to back up what they decide is the answer for people like me. One thing I kept coming across over and over and over again was this idea that I, as the abused child, should aim to forgive my abuser; that I should imagine an apology in my mind and accept it, and move on from there. That really affected me, especially the more I came across it, the more I saw it echoed in books and articles. I felt gaslit, like I was going crazy. I hated Davy. There was nothing in my humanity that could extend to forgiving him for beating my mother, for abusing me, for hurting my sisters too. Why was this being peddled as the way to heal my pain?

I tried, let me tell you that, I did try. I used to practise forgiving him in my mind. I'd say the words out loud. But they were not true, and so that made me feel worse. I felt like I was the bad one now, because I was not capable of forgiveness. I felt inadequate and wrong. I had been okay, but this narrative was pushing me backwards into territory where I was upset and confused again. This man had ruined my childhood, made me live in a state of terror, done unspeakable harm to my body and to my mind. He had destroyed my life, and my mother's and my sisters'.

As I attempted to forgive, over and over again, and saw how much worse that made me feel, I decided that it was a no. This idea was wrong. I did not have to forgive him, I did not have to imagine an apology, because that was living in a lie. I'd done that enough times, I wasn't going to do it now. I hated Davy Tweed. I hated him as a child and I hated him now. I wished him the worst life. He tortured me. He destroyed me. I hated him with every single cell of my body. It was the natural thing to do. That emotion, hate, it exists for a reason. It is instinctive. It is part of the mind's system that helps us survive – we run from the things that hurt us. We avoid them. We hate them. So I allowed this in my life. I allowed myself to hate him and the person who I forgave was myself. My life was far easier when I was honest, I found.

Another thing that struck me when I was learning and educating myself about trauma, was this idea that trauma makes you stronger. I don't believe that. I dismiss that idea as a way to allow abusers to continue on, a passive flattery directed to the abused, telling them they have superpowers because of the abuse. It's disgraceful. I'm not stronger at all. If anything, I have cracks all through me that give way the moment any pressure is put on them. What I have is something I don't want, the ability to keep my emotions inside when I am being tested. That's not a human, it's a sort of robot. I am careful, I never move first, I keep my *self* to myself. That's not living freely, that's not strength.

As a child I was never free, and so I am an adult who never had a childhood. Through the complaint and court case, I discovered a new strength, the strength to stand up against Davy Tweed. I am slowly stepping into the person I was destined to be, I am slowly finding the person I was born to be, the one I was for only three years before I was destroyed. Maybe someday I will merge those two people and feel whole again. Who knows?

Through all of this, through becoming a mother, through the pandemic and its challenges, through my education, I have finally learned to trust my gut. It has never failed me. I used to feel like I could not trust myself because I was being manipulated. In my relationships I was also being abused, all be it mentally. I was told my feelings were crazy, or wrong; I was told that I was the problem, I was causing the issues. And so I believed that and took the blame. But that is not the truth. Now I have faith in my own gut, my own judgement.

28

Acceptance

In 2021 I met a guy. Mark had some trauma too. He was fragile, as was I. Working on myself was still my priority, so we went really slowly, even though there was a strong mutual attraction. I wanted to empower him to take charge of his own healing. We were just friends for the first while, because he had his own trauma and I didn't want to fall into another disastrous relationship where I was giving everything and getting nothing back. Being with someone who sees you at your lowest point and sees a burden, an annoyance, something in the way. That's not love. That's not a relationship either. I'm not really sure what that is, I don't want to even think about that. I always wanted to believe that my previous relationships were with good people, and the issues were just because things were stressful, but I have learned since that's not the truth.

As I healed, I thought back over the relationships in my life, and the struggle and stress that surrounded me, and how I thought it was me. But it wasn't. I also began to admit that I had been in abusive relationships too, just like my mother was, except the abuse was different, not as blatant, and so I denied it and blamed myself for the horrific outbursts and violence. I made excuses, rolled my eyes and said, 'Men!' when my birthday and anniversaries went forgotten. I bought myself gifts to show when asked what I got.

One Valentine's Day I saw a woman on Facebook tag my partner on a small gift she had been given that day and I accepted his word that she was just a friend. I was made to feel guilty for challenging his behaviour with other women that hurt me. Taking another woman up to dance instead of me. Taking photos with other women when he would never take them with me.

I've been given the silent treatment for attempting to lay down boundaries.

I saw photos of him with women where their lipstick is smudged and believed that I was imagining things. When I found other women's jewellery on the living-room floor after I'd been out for the day, I was accused of being psycho and crazy. When I found texts from women, I accepted the answer that it was for a friend. The hairs in our bathroom were my sisters'.

On one occasion I was held down by the throat on the floor while the police were called. When they arrived and saw the scene, they arrested my partner, who had called them. I argued with them that it wasn't domestic abuse, begged them to let him go, told them I had fought him too.

I have cleaned myself up after a tussle, brushed my hair and smoothed my clothing, and told myself it wasn't abuse, it wasn't violence, it was a one-off. And often it was – I was never in a repetitive situation like my mum. I have felt humiliated by things my partner was saying and I've said, 'Ah, he is just drunk' to excuse it. I have sat through verbal abuse and then been told it was 'a joke'.

I have had things thrown at me, skimming past my head with

inches between. Now I wonder what my life would have been had one of those things hit me. Would I be here? Is it luck that I am? A few times I did get hit by flying objects, on the shoulder or back, and then yelled at because I cried.

I have pulled drawers across doorways to stay safe in my own home. I have set my phone to record and gone to bed so I could prove I wasn't crazy when I was woken up to row with and then accused of starting it.

I have been told all of the things I was seeing were wrong and that my childhood trauma meant I could not believe what I was seeing. I have been told that I looked for special treatment because my dad raped me. And when I lashed out and punched him for that line, I was told I was violent.

Being with abusive men, it's so gradual that it's almost like being brainwashed. It's a repeat of the doctrine that you are bad and hard to love, and they are good and you are driving them to these things. When women come from homes where violence was the norm, it's often hard for them to see the wood for the trees. You get broken down slowly and before you can even take a minute to think, you are hounded and harassed and bullied. You start to behave yourself, trying not to upset him. They abuse you, then they love bomb you and transform into the man you tell yourself is the real one. You swear he is good, because he tells you he is; he insists it, repeats it over and over, makes you doubt what you know. He says that you are the one driving him to abuse you. It's your fault.

That's how it works.

Some of the men I've had relationships with were not good men. But I excused it all because it wasn't as bad as what I had seen with my stepfather. He was my measure for a bad man. But now I know that I was so low in myself that I didn't look up for love, I looked down.

I am still learning to distinguish between love and abuse. I'm learning about gaslighting, when someone flat out says something didn't happen that you were a witness to, or a victim of.

'I never laid a hand on you,' one said the night after he pushed me so hard I knocked my head, 'are you losing your marbles or what?'

I'm learning about love bombing.

'The reason I get so angry is only because I love you so much,' one said after screaming abuse into my face.

I'm learning about guilt-tripping.

I'm learning about playing the victim.

'Do you know the slagging I get down the pub for being with you?' one said.

I was so low in myself coming into those relationships, and as I had heard these things all my life, I couldn't tell what they were.

They were abuse.

With Mark, for the first little while we were together, I was secretly waiting for things to unravel and fall apart. But they didn't.

'Ah Jesus Christ,' he said as I finished up the story of losing my Barbies, 'that there is absolutely heartbreaking.'

I remember sitting up in my chair. Realising that even though I was covering the depth of that story with light-heartedness and humour, Mark got it, he saw it. He could see me. That was something I hadn't had before, a partner who loved me so much they even loved the child I was back then and hurt when she hurt.

Then, randomly, a few months later when he was at work on a Saturday a package arrived addressed to him. And when I told him it was there, he came back and said he would make a cup of tea, taking the package with him. A few minutes later he called me in and he was standing there with his hands behind his back.

'Close your eyes and hold out your hands,' he said.

So I did and felt the weight of a small box laid on my hands.

I opened my eyes and saw I was holding the Magic Moves Barbie in her original packaging, as if she was brand new. I was transported right back to my fifth birthday when it had arrived in the post from my own daddy.

When I say I cried and laughed at the same time, I mean it. The little girl inside me was so happy to see Barbie back in her hands that she giggled and squealed, while the adult woman I was cried with the realisation that this was a token of the love I deserved. It was one of those moments when you know it's all alright. Me and her, that little girl who was so cruelly displaced and abused, she was me and I was alright. I wished I could go back. I wished I could change it, but I couldn't. So I cried and laughed instead.

Epilogue

They say what doesn't kill us makes us stronger. But they are wrong. Trauma doesn't build a stronger person, it just teaches us to put up defences. We build walls, fortresses around ourselves and those are hard to break through. Humans deserve to bond and love and be open and honest with each other. Abusers take that away. David Tweed took that away from me. He took an open, honest and sweet child and created a ghost of her in me.

I remember how it felt to be her, I remember the time in my life – all be it in fleeting wisps of memory brought on by smells and sounds and photos – when I was free. I remember fear being something soothed by the ones I had to run to. I can remember the feel of my skin and the breeze whipping up my curls as I was lifted into my father's arms on Browns Bay beach in the sunshine after being chased by my brother and running to my dad. I remember loving the feel of his chest against my side, my bum resting on his arm, his hand on my waist and his kisses on my cheek. I remember a time, fleeting, when men were safe, when their touch was trustworthy.

I was lovely. I was tiny, but I had a huge bursting heart that flowed an energy through me and out into the world.

Davy Tweed stole that from me. Within the space of a couple of years I had gone out of that little girl and I was nowhere. I had no home. I had no mother. I had no body.

Trauma doesn't build a strong person, you cannot frame hurt and pain that way. Life isn't made better by suffering – can we stop this propaganda?

We see someone who came through it, someone who went through abuse and survived it, and we tell ourselves they were 'strong'. So, what, were the ones who didn't survive weak? Is that what we tell ourselves? The ones who turned to alcohol or drugs or suicide, did they 'give in'?

There is no space at all between the ones who made it through and the ones who didn't. For some women the darkness was too much to bear. We are the same. We *are* the same. I'm not here because I am stronger than them. I am just here. That's how my story went, diverted from the path I was on. The person I would have grown into was obliterated and the woman I am now continued down a path that led into darkness.

I've thought a lot about a phrase we are taught, the one that tells us to never speak ill of the dead. It's something that bothers me. Why are the dead free of punishment? Is that fair? Isn't that just another way to silence people? I'm told over and over to move on, to get over it, to forgive. I'll say it again: No. Speaking ill of the dead is my right as a victim. We should be encouraged to speak up and out whenever we can muster the strength, even if it's after our abuser has died. We should be supported and applauded for it, because we all know one thing for sure – it's easier to come forward as a victim of abuse when you see others do it. If my story teaches us nothing except that, I'm happy. The two women who spoke up before me gave me the courage to do it. Even though they lost in court, their victory came through my fight for justice and my victory.

People can't heal unless their wound is clean.

Instantly after Davy died, I saw the tweets start to appear, the 'in sympathies' and the 'deeply saddened'.

Then I got a private message on Facebook: 'Hello Amanda, I'm a reporter doing a piece on Davy Tweed. Ive seen your posts. Would it be possible to have a chat about him. HJ.'

I warned myself to respond later, to think this all through first and not let my heart rule my head. But I knew already, the moment I read his message, that I wanted to tell my story; I wanted to tell every person in Belfast and beyond exactly who the man was that was being remembered in posts and articles across the world. But it wasn't just me in this. There were so many lives that could be turned upside down by the story Hugh wanted me to tell. Even so, my resolve was firm. I wrote back after a minute.

'I wondered how long it would take for you to get in touch.'

Hugh was straight back.

'Would you like to meet for a chat?'

I said I would let him know. But I knew I would talk to him from the moment I saw his message. I knew now was the time to speak ill of the dead, I knew it was time to stomp down all the superstitions and evils of tradition in my town and to stand over the grave of my abuser and spit on it.

My sisters were supportive, they wanted me to go ahead even though they had his surname, even though if I did everyone would know who it was that sat in the court accusing him of abuse. I said I would make sure to not speak for them, just myself.

I knew, and Hugh reassured me, that speaking up would never cause harm, only good. There is a quote I read once – 'Shame dies when stories are told in safe spaces' – and I thought of it then. Was

I safe? Was this city of mine one that would support me if I told the truth? Did it matter?

When I look back on the public persona I had, and probably still have, I think I have always been seen as brave. Someone who can't be walked over, someone who sticks up for herself. I never took a step back when people threatened me; in fact in school I had a 'do your worst' attitude to bullies and to anyone who tried to push me down. People sometimes said things like 'I wouldn't want to cross you,' and I liked it when they said that – I felt safe when they said it. I was being hurt enough.

You see that was not my reality when I got home and was seen for who I really was, because certainly as a child, but also in my relationships, I was being abused and manipulated and controlled. The outside world might have thought I was fierce and fearless, but I was terrified. I was controlled because the ones who saw me for me, they saw how much I needed to belong somewhere, and by the end of it I would be begging for crumbs of compassion.

Is that why victims aren't believed? In my case my role and Davy's role were reversed when we stepped out of the house – he became the hero and I became the villain once we were outside. But that was a lie. Inside we lived the truth.

It makes it harder to talk, it makes it harder to tell. Because you have to let go of your public face; at least that's how it was for me. The brave one who stands up for herself has to admit that she was small and tired and so absolutely frightened.

When I think back, I think of all the adults who could have seen through my bravado and realised something was going on. I remember one time I went into class, only to be thrown out of it before I sat down for not turning in homework that was due.

When I explained that I had been absent, the teacher let me back in, but never once asked me if I was okay, never once asked if everything was okay at home.

So I decided that I would talk. I was my own safe space now, I was the one who would not be ashamed any more.

When the Sunday morning after I had been interviewed arrived and I knew my story was out there, I woke early with knots in my stomach. Lorraine rang.

'Ah Mo, I am so so proud,' she said, 'grab me a paper too will you?'

My partner Mark was in the kitchen when I went in.

'Tea?' he said.

I shook my head. 'Will you go get two of the paper?' I asked him.

'No problem,' he said and grabbed his coat. 'Need anything else?'

'No, just the paper, thank you,' I said and sat down.

As soon as he went out the door, I felt as though I was going to be sick. I had to steady myself with my hands against the table.

It seemed like forever until he came back and my imagination ran away with itself. Would people call out terrible names my way on the street, would they shout terrible things? Liar, Liar! Should I have done this at all?

Mark came back through the door with a cheerful slam, calling out to me, 'Your wee face is on the cover!'

He held it up: 'My Hell with Paedo Tweed', read the headline.

I don't think I breathed at all as I read the story Hugh had written, but I got through it and exhaled with a large sigh.

'It's what I wanted,' I said, almost to myself. 'It's good.'

Almost immediately messages started to trickle in. By the end of the day they were pouring in on every platform, messages from friends and from strangers. I would love to say it was mostly supportive, but there was some negativity and some cruelty. That was what I had expected.

Radio stations invited me on and I went. My sisters shared their stories too. The more I talked the more I felt a power I hadn't had before. A power to speak ill of the dead, a power to smash all the things I had been conditioned to believe. A power that surged up inside of me and spoke to me. I could make a difference.

What I did notice was that because Davy was dead, people felt unwilling to engage in the destruction of his reputation. As if being dead somehow should wipe his slate clean, as if the dirt and filth he picked up along his own journey was washed away in that moment when he hit the road. I noticed people stumbling and fumbling with words about him, trying to desperately find words that wouldn't offend. Local Unionist politicians praised him after he died but stepped back apologetically when reminded that he was a wife-beater and a child molester.

However, one man did not. A TUV member was pushed on his sympathetic tweet to Davy's family and responded with 'Conviction overturned on appeal but never mind the facts ...'

It hit me like a slap. I physically reeled when I saw it. The word trigger is overused nowadays, but I know what a real trigger is. I felt it then, at that moment when I read that tweet. Like a gunshot going off inside my body, I was plunged into stress, returned to the little girl who wanted to tell but couldn't out of this fear, this exact fear – they don't believe me.

I felt the ground under my feet shift. The knot in my stomach twisted back into place. The relief I had felt briefly was gone. Tweed still had power. He was still here. I would never get rid of him.

This party leader argued that Davy Tweed was an innocent man. He used that word, innocent.

'Sure, you can say what you like about the dead,' he said, in response to the child abuse conviction.

I felt anger in my stomach where the anxiety had been before. I paced the floor, ranted. I took to Twitter.

'He was acquitted,' he tweeted.

I wanted to scream. After all of the pain and trauma, after the years of getting myself to the point of being finally able to live, this man was pointing at me and saying that I wasn't to be believed.

Davy was never acquitted. He managed to argue a legal point successfully and have his conviction quashed. That was a technicality.

I considered writing this politician a private email, but after I saw him interviewed on the BBC and the way he spoke about Davy, I decided to send him an open letter. My power would not be quashed by this man. I would not sit down. I would stand up for myself and I would stand up for women.

My tweet started to move. Within twenty-four hours my letter had 10,000 views. My phone was pinging so much I had to turn it off. I was being tagged in retweets and quote tweets and shared all over.

An apology arrived the next day.

My bad feelings were soon washed away by the wave of support that followed. I got texts and tweets and emails from other survivors of abuse who told me that they felt less alone because of my story. By speaking up I was validating them. I was helping people.

That's what these stories do. They say 'you are not alone' to people who feel that way. These stories can echo other people's own stories and help them understand what happened to them a bit more. It can help them get to a point where they believe that it was not their fault. No matter what way we are conditioned, or how society and our culture tells us that women are to blame for men's rage and men's violence and men's lust, we can speak up and speak together until we are so loud that nobody can ignore us. And things will change then. Things *will* change then.

Abusers rely on silence. They rely on society to protect them by keeping this topic difficult to broach. Abusers rely on society to assume first that the victim is lying.

We have to show proper support for victims and move the starting point to believing victims. People think that means we take the word of anyone, but it doesn't. What it means is that the starting point is belief and not suspicion. The first place they come to should be a place where they are believed; that should be the message to all victims: we will believe you.

No matter how long ago, no matter how little you can recall, we will believe you.

If we do that, we will light up the darkness. We will force child abusers out of the shadows in which they hide, where they frighten and hurt children.

We have to take a stand against silence. Because the power of enforced silence is stronger than anything.

Yes, you can say what you like about the dead, but what you say should reflect their truth, not a made-up fairy tale.

So I will speak the truth. I will tell my story. I will speak ill of the dead.

I will.

Davy Tweed was a wife-beater.

Davy Tweed was a child molester.

Davy Tweed was a monster.

Acknowledgements

Thank you, Hugh Jordan, for breaking this story in the press and by doing so, showing me the power that comes from sharing my truth. This book would not be here without you.

I'd like to thank my sisters, Lorraine, Catherine, Victoria and Jamiee-Leigh, for all of their support and love through the hardest times of our lives. Also thanks to my wonderful mother, Margaret, and to my extended family and friends for always looking out for me and for standing up with me against the ignorance of others. Mark, thank you for your patience and compassion, and for holding space for me, and for cheering me on as I have navigated these past few years. To my closest friends for believing in me when I didn't and taking on the roles of confidants and counsellors during the aftermath. A special thanks to Pauline, who has proven to be my number one fan.

Thanks to Merrion Press, the publishing team, Conor Graham, Wendy Logue, and my editor Liosa McNamara for everything you have done.

Finally, and most importantly, thank you to my wee son, Grayson, for the love and light you have brought to my life and for giving up your time with Mummy while she wrote this book.